Filmmaker's Dictionary

by

Ralph S. Singleton

LONE EAGLE

To Helen P. Singleton and Gio Coppola

FILMMAKERS DICTIONARY

Copyright © 1986 by Ralph S. Singleton

LONE EAGLE PUBLISHING CO.
9903 Santa Monica Blvd. #204
Beverly Hills, CA 90212
213/471-8066

Printed in the United States of America

Graphic Design by Gloriane Harris

Library of Congress Cataloging in Publication Data

Singleton, Ralph S. (Ralph Stuart), 1940-
    FILMMAKER'S DICTIONARY.

    1. Moving-pictures -- Dictionaries. 2. Cinematography --
Dictionaries. 3. Television -- Dictionaries. I. Title.
PN1993.45.S56 1986   791.43'03   86-15303
ISBN 0-943728-08-8

90 89 88 87 86

10 9 8 7 6 5 4 3 2 1

Words in CAPITAL LETTERS are defined elsewhere in the Filmmaker's Dictionary.

NOTE: We have made every reasonable effort to ensure that the information contained herein is as accurate as possible. However, errors and omissions are sure to occur. We would appreciate your notifying us of any which you may find.

ACKNOWLEDGMENTS

EXTERIOR - School - 1969 - Night
David Moon (art director) and I sat talking in the deserted bleachers. I listened with fascination as he told me that if I planned a career in the motion picture industry, I'd better understand what some of the terms meant. He started with *Gaffer* and *Best Boy*. This book actually began that evening. Thank you, David.

I would also like to thank all the people who contributed their "ten words," the people I plagued for "just one more definition," the technical advisors and experts in their own fields who added words and terms to help make this dictionary so complete, and to those tireless people who proofread our "final" versions...only to have us add more words. To name every single person would fill another book, so I shall name just a few: Jim Ruxin, Bob Shure and "the guys" at CFI, Norman Rudman, Esq., James Turner, George Willig, Jack Jennings, Edward Plante, Dick Reilly, Barbara Rosing, Toti Levine, Paul Stubenrauch, Randy Morgan, Steve Dawson, Rob Mendel, Elizabeth Vietor, Carol MacConaugha, Patrice Klinger, Rob Newman, Mar Elepano from the USC Film Lab, Panavision, and our friends at the Academy of Motion Picture Arts & Sciences Margaret Herrick Library and the AFI Library.

A special word of thanks to a very special friend, Lois Anne Polan. Without her persistence and determination, the *Filmmaker's Dictionary* would still be sitting in the computer, waiting to be edited.

And, of course, my gratitude and appreciation to my editor and publisher (and now my wife), Joan E. Vietor.

Ralph S. Singleton
Los Angeles, California

FOREWORD

"An INDIE PROD with a FIVE PIC PACK is BICYCLING between his DEVELOPMENT DEAL at one STUDIO and his MOW commitment at a MAJOR WEB, hoping that when he TAKES A MEETING this afternoon, he will be able to STRIKE A DEAL with the TALENT before his first project goes into TURNAROUND." "If we finish this SCENE before lunch, we can avoid a MEAL PENALTY and have time to SCREEN THE DAILIES."

Roughly translated, the first sentence says, "An independent producer who has a deal to do five pictures is juggling his time between one project which is in development at a major studio and a Movie of the Week project which he is doing for a television network, in the hopes that he will be able to successfully finish negotiations with the main stars before the studio decides not to do the project." The second sentence says," If we finish filming this particular piece before lunch, we will not have to pay the cast and crew members extra by making them wait to have their lunch, and be able to view the film we shot yesterday."

Each industry has its own particular language, special terms, and jargon. It would be impossible to put down every word that is used in the motion picture industry, and so I have chosen to limit it to the ones I feel are the most widely-used. That is not to say that you won't find some real unusual terms, though. *"Murder your wife" brick* is one that was new to me, and I've been working in this business for over sixteen years. I also hope you appreciate the touches of humor here and there. It's impossible to write about the "industry" without a slight smile.

For the industry professional, *Filmmaker's Dictionary* will help you understand terms that are not in your field. For the student or novice filmmaker, it should provide you with a good foundation of knowledge so you won't react in horror when someone asks you to "kill the baby." You'll know that all they meant was to turn off the small spotlight.

Happy filmmaking!

A

A AND B CUTTING *(aka A AND B ROLLING)*
A NEGATIVE CUTTING technique used in 16mm to make invisible
SPLICES. The first SHOT is put onto the A roll, with black
LEADER in the corresponding position on the B roll. The second shot
is then put onto the B roll, with black leader in the corresponding
position on the A roll. All subsequent shots are checkerboarded
(alternated) with black leader in the same manner. The two rolls are
then printed separately onto the STOCK of the next GENERATION so
that the shots touch each other with no splice in between. This is not
necessary in 35mm because the FRAME is so much larger that a splice
does not show.

A and B cutting is used in both 16mm and 35mm to make FADES
and DISSOLVES that are not done by an OPTICAL HOUSE. For a
dissolve or SUPERIMPOSITION, two shots are overlapped *(aka LAP
DISSOLVE)* on the A and B rolls. More rolls (C, D, etc.) can be used
for additional superimpositions, TITLES, etc.

A AND B ROLLING
See A AND B CUTTING.

ABBY SINGER SHOT
Production jargon for the next-to-the-last shot of the day *(e.g., "The next
shot is the Abby Singer.")* The term came into use when Mr. Singer
was an ASSISTANT DIRECTOR.

1

ABERRATION, LENS
An imperfection in a lens that causes a distorted IMAGE.

ABOVE-THE-LINE *(sometimes abbr. ATL)*
A film's BUDGET is divided into two main sections: Above-the-line and BELOW-THE-LINE. Above-the line expenditures are usually negotiated on a RUN OF SHOW basis and, generally, are the most expensive individual items on the budget *(e.g., costs for Story and Screenplay, PRODUCER, DIRECTOR, and CAST.)* Below-the-line costs consist of the technicians, materials and labor. Labor costs are usually calculated on a daily basis. Also included in below-the-line costs are: RAW STOCK, PROCESSING, equipment, STAGE space and all other PRODUCTION and POST PRODUCTION costs.

ABOVE THE TITLE
This refers to the position of FRONT CREDITS that appear before the MAIN TITLE of the film. The order of credits is usually as follows: DISTRIBUTOR, PRODUCER/PRODUCTION COMPANY, that presents a (name of DIRECTOR) film, followed by name or names of principal STAR/S, then the film title. Recently, more and more credits appear above the title. In previous days, however, this space was carefully guarded, with only the name of the distributor, and perhaps a particularly powerful producer appearing *(e.g., David O. Selznick, Samuel Goldwyn, Dino De Laurentiis)* . Frank Capra was the first director to have his name above the title. *See also BILLING, TOP BILLING.*

ABRASIONS
Damage to film caused by improper handling or winding. These usually show up as cuts and scratches on the processed film's surface.

ACADEMY AWARDS *(aka OSCARS)*
Honors presented every Spring by members of the ACADEMY OF MOTION PICTURE ARTS AND SCIENCES (AMPAS) for artistic and technical achievement in various categories of the motion picture industry. The first Awards were presented in 1927.

ACADEMY LEADER
The ACADEMY OF MOTION PICTURE ARTS AND SCIENCES (AMPAS) designated leader (black film). It is attached to the HEAD of each REEL and has numbers from ten to two in descending order to show where the picture starts. At the number *two*, there is a beep that is a sound CUE (signifying that the picture is about to start), and then the picture begins where the number *one* would be. A newer system,

designed by the SOCIETY OF MOTION PICTURE AND TELEVISION ENGINEERS (SMPTE) for use in theatrical and television PROJECTION of motion pictures, is called UNIVERSAL LEADER.

ACADEMY OF MOTION PICTURE ARTS AND SCIENCES *(Abbr. AMPAS)*
An honorary organization of filmmakers whose membership is by invitation only. The over 3000 members are divided into different branches according to category *(e.g., DIRECTORS, ACTORS, CINEMATOGRAPHERS, ART DIRECTORS, COMPOSERS)*. Each year they vote on and present the ACADEMY AWARDS (OSCARS) for artistic and technical achievement in the motion picture industry. Each branch votes on the nominees in their own category, and the entire membership votes for Best Picture.

ACCELERATED MOTION
ACTION shot with the camera running at a speed of less than 24 FRAMES PER SECOND (normal sound speed) so that when PROJECTED at normal speed, it appears speeded-up. The opposite is SLOW MOTION.

A.C.E.
Abbreviation for AMERICAN CINEMA EDITORS. An honorary professional society of film EDITORS. Membership is by invitation only.

ACE
A 1000-watt SPOT equipped with a FRESNEL LENS.

ACETATE BASE *(aka SAFETY BASE)*
A slow-burning, chemical film base that has replaced the older, highly-flammable NITRATE BASE. Most older films have been TRANSFERRED to the more durable acetate base.

ACTION
Movement in front of the camera.

ACTION!
What the DIRECTOR says when he/she wishes the movement/DIALOGUE in a SCENE to commence.

ACTION STILL
A photograph BLOWN UP from an actual FRAME of a motion picture, as opposed to a photograph taken with a STILL camera.

ACTION TRACK
The film (picture) before any music, DIALOGUE or EFFECTS TRACKS are added.

ACTOR/ACTRESS
Any person who performs in a play, television show, film, etc. Anyone working on a UNION film or television project who utters one word is said to have a *speaking part* , and must be paid according to the rules and regulations of the SCREEN ACTORS GUILD (SAG). PRODUCTIONS on tape (audio or video) are under the jurisdiction of the American Federation of Television and Radio Artists (AFTRA). Theatrical productions fall under the jurisdiction of ACTORS EQUITY *(see EQUITY)*.

ACTOR'S TIME SHEET
A daily record of the times an actor works, when meal breaks or meal penalties, occurred and for how long, and at what time he/she was released. The actor signs his record each day and then a copy is sent to SAG (or AFTRA).

AD
Abbreviation for ASSISTANT DIRECTOR. *See FIRST ASSISTANT DIRECTOR, SECOND ASSISTANT DIRECTOR.*

ADAPTATION
A SCREENPLAY whose story comes from another medium, such as a novel, short story, magazine article, etc.

ADDED SCENE
An additional scene inserted into a SCRIPT that has already been assigned SCENE NUMBERS. The added scene is noted with a letter beside the number. *See also OMITTED SCENE, A-PAGE.*

AD LIB
Extemporaneous DIALOGUE that does not appear in the SCRIPT. *See also IMPROVISE, WING IT.*

ADR
Abbreviation for Automatic Dialogue Replacement. *See also LOOPING, DUBBING, ELECTRONIC LINE REPLACEMENT.*

ADVANCE
The number of FRAMES by which the sound recording must precede the film IMAGE in order to be IN SYNC. For 35mm, the advance is 20 FRAMES, and for 16mm, 26 frames.

AERIAL SHOT
A SCENE filmed from a helicopter or plane, etc., using a special CAMERA MOUNT. *See 'COPTER MOUNT, TYLER MOUNT.*

AFI
Abbreviation for the AMERICAN FILM INSTITUTE.

AFM
Abbreviation for American Federation of Musicians, the musicians UNION.

AFTRA
Abbreviation for AMERICAN FEDERATION OF TELEVISION AND RADIO ARTISTS.

AGENT
A person or company licensed by the state to represent clients and negotiate contracts on their behalf. The standard agent's fee is ten percent of the client's salary. Some of the more well-known talent agencies are: the William Morris Agency, International Creative Management *(ICM)*, Creative Artists Agency *(CAA)*.

AIR-TO-AIR
Used to describe a SHOT of a flying object taken from another flying object, such as a helicopter or plane.

ALLIGATOR CLAMPS
Small, pointed spring clips, so-called because they resemble an alligator's jaws. They are used on a SET to temporarily hold things in place during PRODUCTION.

AMBIENCE
Mood, feeling or presence that is the desired EFFECT in a SCENE.

AMBIENT SOUND
Normal sounds that exist in a particular place *(e.g., street noise, chirping birds, wind, ROOM TONE.)*

AMERICAN CINEMA EDITORS *(Abbr. A.C.E.)*
An honorary professional society of film EDITORS. Membership is by invitation only.

AMERICAN FEDERATION OF TELEVISION AND RADIO ARTISTS *(Abbr. AFTRA)*
This is the television/radio/videotape counterpart of the SCREEN ACTORS GUILD.

AMERICAN FILM INSTITUTE *(Abbr. AFI)*
The activities of the AFI include a film school, a FILM ARCHIVE, film preservation and restoration, oral histories of people in the film business, and the designation and presentation of a Life Achievement award each year. It is partially financed by the National Endowment for the Arts.

AMERICAN SOCIETY OF CINEMATOGRAPHERS *(Abbr. A.S.C.)*
An honorary group whose members are some of the best cinematographers in America. The British counterpart is the British Society of Cinematographers (B.S.C.), and the Canadian counterpart is the Canadian Society of Cinematographers (C.S.C.)

AMORTIZE, AMORTIZATION
To reduce and finally settle a debt by regular, periodic payments of principal and interest. In the case of motion pictures, the NEGATIVE COST is charged against revenue, thereby lowering the debt.

AMPAS
Abbreviation for ACADEMY OF MOTION PICTURE ARTS AND SCIENCES.

ANAMORPHIC LENS
A lens used when photographing in WIDE SCREEN onto standard 35mm film STOCK. The wide screen SHOT is compressed by the lens so that it fits into the standard FRAME, then is PROJECTED through another anamorphic lens to unsqueeze it and return it to wide screen proportions.

ANGLE, CAMERA
The point of view (POV) of the camera when it is set up for SHOOTING. Camera angles are chosen for a variety of reasons - never haphazardly. The angle determines how the viewer will see the characters and action and can be used to emphasize one or more

characters, set a mood, single out an object to give it additional importance, etc.

ANIMAL HANDLER
See WRANGLER.

ANIMATION
A specialized branch of filmmaking whereby drawings or three-dimensional objects are photographed FRAME by frame (most commonly two frames at a time and sometimes, low BUDGET PRODUCTIONS, three frames) so that when they are PROJECTED at a normal speed the illusion of movement is created. Sometimes (in art films) drawing or painting is done directly on the film.

ANIMATION BED
A specially designed table that is used with an ANIMATION STAND. It has pegs that hold the ANIMATION CEL being photographed, and can be turned so that the artwork, as well as the camera, can move. There are top and bottom lights on the bed.

ANIMATION CAMERA
A camera capable of shooting FRAME by frame. Used in ANIMATION.

ANIMATION CEL
A piece of transparent acetate, approximately 9x12 inches, that contains one in a series of drawings to be photographed for an animated film. Formerly, each cel was drawn by hand. Today, the outlines are drawn onto paper, then transferred onto acetate, after which the colors are filled in by hand.

ANIMATION STAND
An elaborately designed and constructed unit that holds the ANIMATION CAMERA rigidly in place. It regulates the movement of the camera by calibration and allows for ZOOMS.

ANIMATOR
The artist who draws or constructs objects to be animated.

ANKLE
A TRADE PAPER term meaning to be voluntarily no longer associated with (a project, a company).

ANSWER PRINT

The first COMPOSITE (sound and picture) PRINT that the LAB sends for approval. It sometimes takes several answer prints before all the required color corrections are made and STRUCK. Sometimes answer prints are silent *(e.g., if the MIX hasn't been completed.)*

ANTI-HALATION

A transparent coating applied to the CEL SIDE of the NEGATIVE to reduce HALATION - any unwanted FLARES or halos on the film. It is removed during PROCESSING.

A-PAGE

An additional page inserted in a SCRIPT between two already numbered pages. Subsequent additional pages inserted after that particular page before the next number are lettered A,B,C, etc. *(e.g., 127, 127A, 127B, 128.) See also BLUE PAGES.*

APERTURE

The opening in a LENS that controls the amount of light passing through the CAMERA, PROJECTOR, or PRINTER. The size of the aperture is calibrated in F-STOPS and is regulated by the DIAPHRAGM. *See also DEPTH OF FIELD.*

APERTURE PLATE

A rectangular mask in front of the film in a camera. It defines the FRAME by blocking light from the edges of the film.

APOCHROMATIC LENS

A lens that corrects for CHROMATIC ABERRATION in color photography by causing the light rays of different wave lengths to converge at a single point.

APPLE BOX

A standard size wooden crate used to raise the height of people, lights, PROPS, etc., during shooting. There are also HALF- and QUARTER-APPLES.

APPRENTICE EDITOR

The member of the EDITING staff who handles miscellaneous tasks while learning the different responsibilities of EDITOR and ASSISTANT EDITOR.

ARBITRATION

A forum for resolving disputes through an informal, non-judicial hearing. Participants in an arbitration agree to be bound by the decision of the board or individual hearing the arbitration for the resolution of claims.

ARC

1) A high-intensity lamp that operates on direct current. The two types are: Xenon/MERCURY ARCS, which require no adjustment, and Carbon Arcs, which require frequent adjustment. Carbon Arcs produce light that approximate daylight (around 4800 Kelvin), so are often used to simulate sunlight in the STUDIO, and as boosters for outdoor color shooting. 2) The progression of various plots as they are woven through the story. In serial television, it relates to the plans for the various characters during the season.

ARRANGER

The person who prepares and adapts previously written music for presentation in some form other than its original form. Often an arranger will work from a COMPOSER'S sketch and create parts that will then be assigned to various voices and/or instruments by the ORCHESTRATOR. Sometimes the composer does his/her own arranging and orchestrating. In the pop music idiom, the arranger and orchestrator are the same person. Often, in more legitimate music (film, symphony, etc.) the term orchestrator is used.

ARRESTED, CAN'T GET

Slang meaning to not be able to get a job (*e.g., I have gone out on six auditions this week and I can't get arrested!*)

ARRIFLEX *(aka ARRI)*

A brand of motion picture camera. The Arri was the first portable, SELF-BLIMPED 35mm movie camera.

ART DEPARTMENT

The crew members who, under the direction of the PRODUCTION DESIGNER, are responsible for creating the *look* of a film as far as SETS and LOCATIONS are concerned. (The CAMERAMAN and COSTUME DESIGNER also contribute to the overall *look* of a film.) The staff usually includes the ART DIRECTOR, an ASSISTANT ART DIRECTOR, SET DESIGNER, Draftsman and Apprentice.

ART DIRECTOR

The person who supervises and is responsible for every aspect of the film's decor and SET construction. He must be knowledgeable in architecture, design, etc. *See also PRODUCTION DESIGNER.*

ARTIFICIAL BREAKEVEN
A mutually agreed-upon amount of revenue generated by a film which, when reached, triggers the payment of some PROFITS. *See also BREAKEVEN.*

ARTIFICIAL LIGHT
The opposite of natural light. Any man-made light from FLOODS, SPOTLIGHTS, etc.

ASA SPEED RATING
An internationally accepted system for identifying the IMAGE recording ability (EMULSION SPEED) of film. The higher the ASA number, the more sensitive the emulsion. Other rating systems are DIN, the European standard, and ISO, the newest system, also used internationally.

A.S.C.
Abbreviation for AMERICAN SOCIETY OF CINEMATOGRAPHERS.

A-SCENE
See ADDED SCENE.

ASPECT RATIO
The relationship, width-to-height, of a projected or printed motion picture FRAME. There are several different aspect ratios used: Academy aperture - 1.33:1, Standard - 1.85:1, and WIDE SCREEN - 2.35:1. Television is proportionately the same as Academy. An interesting note: The range of vision of the human eye is an ellipse whose proportions are roughly 1.85 to 1. *See also SCREEN, WIDE SCREEN PROCESS, CINEMASCOPE, CINERAMA.*

ASSEMBLY
The first step of EDITING when SCENES are put together in SCRIPT sequence, to roughly tell the story. *See also ROUGH CUT, FINE CUT, FINAL CUT, EDITING.*

ASSISTANT CAMERAMAN
See FIRST ASSISTANT CAMERAMAN and SECOND ASSISTANT CAMERAMAN.

ASSISTANT DIRECTOR *(Abbr. AD)*
See FIRST ASSISTANT DIRECTOR, SECOND ASSISTANT DIRECTOR, KEY SECOND A.D., SECOND SECOND.

ASSISTANT EDITOR
The member of the EDITING staff who works with the EDITOR to SYNCS DAILIES, catalogues and keeps the dailies organized and accessible, splices film, and keeps the EDITING ROOM in working order. Having a good filing and coding system aids in keeping track of the thousands of feet of film. The Assistant Editor talks with the labs and effects companies and, in general, relieves the Editor of having to do jobs other than editing.

ASSOCIATE DIRECTOR
Production position in a live or taped television show whose duties include assisting the DIRECTOR with anything he/she needs; telling the department heads what the director wants before taping begins; communicating with the Stage Manager and cameras to make sure they know the director's instructions; making sure cameras are in position during taping before the director calls the SHOTS, and keeping a log of the tape during taping.

ASSOCIATE PRODUCER
A title that varies from PRODUCTION to production. It can be the title given to the PRODUCER'S second-in-command who shares business and creative responsibilities, or it can designate an additional credit given to the PRODUCTION MANAGER (the actual LINE PRODUCER when the PRODUCER is not always directly involved with the production on a daily basis) or be an honorary title given to one of the financiers, or the person responsible for bringing the property to the producer.

ASTIGMATISM
A LENS imperfection, whose effects can sometimes be corrected or lessened by STOPPING THE LENS DOWN (*i.e., decreasing the size of the APERTURE.*)

ASYNCHRONISM
A discrepancy between the SOUND TRACK and the IMAGE on the SCREEN. *See IN SYNC, OUT OF SYNC, SYNCHRONIZATION.*

ATMOSPHERE
1) The main emotional theme or mood of a film or SCENE or,
2) EXTRAS in a scene who lend a sense of realism to the action.

ATMOSPHERE VEHICLE
Any car, truck, motorcycle, etc., that is used in a SCENE on the PRODUCTION and is not used by PRINCIPAL PLAYERS or any other actor with a SPEAKING PART.

AUDIO
Anything related to the sound portion of the film or tape, as opposed to the VIDEO, or visual, portion.

AUDIT
A formal examination, reconciliation and verification of all financial accounts and records. This may apply to PRODUCTION auditing or DISTRIBUTION auditing (of revenues generated by the film).

AUDITION
An actor's or actress' test, or READING, for a part in a film or play.

AUDITOR
The person responsible for keeping the financial records, issuing COST REPORTS, estimating final costs, etc., for a film. *See also PRODUCTION ACCOUNTANT, LOCATION AUDITOR.*

AVAILABLE LIGHT
Natural light. This term refers to shooting without adding ARTIFICIAL LIGHT.

A-WIND
Film STOCK wound with the EMULSION side down, generally used for PROJECTION and PRINTING on POSITIVE GENERATIONS *(i.e., INTERPOSITIVE)* between the ORIGINAL NEGATIVE and RELEASE PRINTS. *See also B-WIND, WIND.*

B

BABY
See BABY SPOT.

BABY LEGS *(aka SHORTY, BABY TRIPOD)*
A short camera stand (TRIPOD) used for shooting from low angles. It is the smallest of the three tripods.

BABY SPOT *(aka BABY, BABY KEG)*
A spotlight, smaller than a JUNIOR. Usually takes a 500 or 750-watt lamp.

BACKER
Financier. A person who puts up money for a show or a film.

BACKERS' AUDITION
A performance of a show which is done in workshop form and presented specifically for an audience of potential BACKERS.

BACKGROUND *(Abbr. BG)*
1) The part of the SCENE that is furthest away from the camera and still in view. 2) The real or artificial setting in front of which the ACTION in a scene takes place. 3) EXTRAS used for background action or ambience *(aka ATMOSPHERE)*.

BACKGROUND NOISE
Sounds that give the illusion of action OFF CAMERA or general ambience *(e.g., car honk, muffled voices, a train whistle, a clock chiming, frogs croaking)* that are added to the SOUND TRACK in POST-PRODUCTION. *See also WILD* SOUND.

BACKGROUND LIGHTING
See LIGHTING.

BACKING *(aka BACKDROP)*
A painted or photographic rendering used to give the illusion of a real BACKGROUND, such as the view through a door or window, or natural setting on a interior SET.

BACKLIGHT
The technique of lighting a subject from behind, (relative to camera position) creating a silhouette or halo effect.

BACK LOT
An open-air part of a STUDIO where EXTERIORS may be shot. There are usually many different STANDING SETS *(e.g., Old New York, Western Town, Modern City)*. Studios save a great deal of money by not having to build new, elaborate sets.

BACK PROJECTION
See REAR SCREEN PROJECTION, PROCESS SHOT.

BACK-UP SCHEDULE *(aka COVER SET)*
An alternate film LOCATION and timetable which can be used in the event that shooting cannot proceed as planned. Often, exterior shooting is thwarted by weather, so it is imperative to have a back-up schedule of interior shooting which can be substituted.

BAFFLE
1) A sound-absorbing screen inside a loud-speaker which improves fidelity by increasing and decreasing reverberation. 2) A microphone attachment which accentuates high frequencies. 3) A sound-absorbing, movable wall used to prevent reverberation in studio recording *(aka Baffle Blanket)*. 4) A studio lamp SHUTTER that directs and controls light intensity.

BALANCE
1) When referring to LIGHTING, it is the relationship between the KEY LIGHT and FILL LIGHT. 2) When referring to sound, it is the relative volume of the DIALOGUE, MUSIC and EFFECTS

TRACKS, or, in the music channel the relative volume of instruments and/or vocals. 3) It can also refer to the total composition of a SHOT so that it is eye-pleasing and not lopsided.

BALANCED PRINT
A print that has been COLOR CORRECTED or GRADED.

BALANCING STRIPE
A MAGNETIC STRIPE applied to the film edge opposite the magnetic sound stripe. This keeps the thickness of the film uniform on both sides when it is wound. It protects against damage to the film's surface.

BANANA
To walk in a curved arc in front of the camera so as to stay IN FOCUS.

BANK
A financial institution which may lend money for DEVELOPMENT, PRODUCTION, POST-PRODUCTION, etc., of a FEATURE FILM based on certain GUARANTEES, *(e.g., pre-sales, DISTRIBUTION agreements).* An investor in a production puts up money and receives a certain percentage of the PROFITS after RECOUPING his investment, or may lose the whole investment if the project fails. A bank only lends money, does not usually take a percentage, but makes its money on the INTEREST charged.

BANK *(aka COOPS)*
A large number of lamps mounted in a single housing, used for illuminating large areas.

BARN DOORS
Folding metal gates on lamps that help direct and control the light.

BARNEY *(aka BLIMP)*
A heavily-insulated, yet flexible cover that fits over an un-blimped camera to deaden camera noise during SYNCHRONIZED filming, or to protect the camera from the elements (*e.g., extreme temperatures, rain).*

BASE
Smooth, thin, transparent film onto which light sensitive EMULSION or magnetic recording substance is coated. Since 1952, a slow-burning SAFETY or ACETATE BASE has replaced the

highly-flammable NITRATE BASE which was used previously. *See also CELLULOID.*

BASHER
A small, low-powered lamp that is used as a FLOODLIGHT or SPOT. It may be either hand-held or fixed.

BATCH NUMBER
The film manufacturer's code, designating the time of preparation of that EMULSION. It was usually advisable to use STOCK from the same batch when shooting a particular SEQUENCE, so as to assure consistent color and emulsion speed. These days, however, PROCESSING has become so sophisticated that differences in emulsion can be corrected in the LAB, so stock from different batches can be used together. *See also EMULSION NUMBER, EMULSION SPEED.*

BATTERIES
Portable energy source. Sometimes on LOCATION, it is impossible to bring in power, so batteries must be used to run the equipment. There are three basic types of batteries: Wet Cell - rechargeable, but bulky; Dry Cell - non-rechargeable with a limited life-span, but portable; Nickel Cadmium - long life, resistant to high and low temperatures and requires little maintenance, but are more expensive.

BATTERY BELT
A compact, portable energy source worn by the CAMERA OPERATOR around his/her waist. The camera is plugged into the battery belt, thus giving the operator maximum mobility. This is used primarily for LOCATION newsreel shooting and DOCUMENTARIES.

BAZOOKA
A STUDIO light support for use on a CATWALK.

BEAT
Writer's slang for the main storyline, or "heartbeat" of a story.

BEAT SHEET
Writer's term for a page or two containing one- or two-line summaries of stories. Usually used in episodic or serial television.

BELLY BOARD
A small platform for mounting a camera as close to ground level as possible.

BELOW-THE-LINE *(Abbr. BTL)*
See ABOVE-THE-LINE.

BEST BOY
Two separate positions: second in command to tbe GAFFER and to the KEY GRIP. The Best Boy/Grip is in charge of the rest of the grips and grip equipment; the Best Boy/Electric is in charge of the rest of the electricians and the electrical equipment.

BG
Abbreviation for BACKGROUND.

BIBLE RUN
The complete, updated weekly computer run of all accounting activity on a motion picture PRODUCTION.

BICYCLE
A slang term meaning to work on more than one project at a time.

BICYCLE A PRINT
In order to be able to SCREEN what is sometimes the only print of a film to more than one audience at the same time *(e.g., STUDIO executives in different SCREENING ROOMS watching a ROUGH CUT)* a messenger on a bicycle waits outside thc PROJECTION BOOTH to receive each REEL as it is completed, then bicycles it to the next screening room. This is also the term used when rotating prints from one play date (theatre) to another around the country.

BILLING
The placement of names, titles, etc., in the CREDITS. In addition to salary and POINTS in a film, billing is a major issue when negotiating a DEAL. Size of credit (in relationship to the MAIN TITLE and other performers or crew members) and placement on the SCREEN, how many other names are on the CARD, etc., are all considered, and if not found to be satisfactory, can be considered a DEAL BREAKER. Most GUILD/UNION contracts spell out billing clauses.

BIN *(aka TRIM BIN)*
A wheeled container, usually made of fire resistant cloth, which holds film that is being EDITED. It has a frame on the top with small hooks on which film can be hung.

BINAURAL REPRODUCTION
A two-channel sound system which closely approximates sound heard by the human ear. Three or more channels are generally referred to as STEREOPHONIC reproduction.

BINOCULAR VISION
Vision which has DEPTH OF FIELD resulting from viewing an object through two separate viewfinders (*i.e., human eyes*). The resulting, overlapping IMAGES allow the viewer to judge distances and sizes. While most films' images are planoscopic (flat), 3-D films are stereophonic and try to approximate binocular vision.

BIPACK PRINTING
A film duplicating process used in MATTE SHOTS or for intentional DOUBLE EXPOSURES where two pieces of film are PRINTED simultaneously.

BIT/BIT PLAYER
A small speaking part--usually two or three lines. Not to be confused with SILENT BITS.

BLACKS
CLOTHS or DRAPES used to block daylight from windows or doorways when shooting Night Interiors, or to create the illusion of night when shooting a small, Night Exterior. An interesting exception: large portions of Universal Studios' back lot were blacked out when shooting *STREETS OF FIRE* as it was less expensive than shooting NIGHT FOR NIGHT.

BLACK TRACK PRINT
A silent (no sound, just picture) ANSWER PRINT.

BLANK
Ammunition that contains paper or plastic in place of the bullet.

BLEACHED OUT (aka BURNT UP)
Film exposed to too much light so that all detail is lost.

BLIMP
Soundproof housing for the camera, usually made of magnesium lined with rubber and plastic foam. The camera can be operated with the blimp in place. *See also BARNEY.*

BLIND BIDDING
A controversial practice, illegal in many states, whereby a DISTRIBUTOR requires an EXHIBITOR to bid on, and eventually commit to exhibit films prior to seeing them.

BLOCK BOOKING
A controversial practice whereby a DISTRIBUTOR requires an EXHIBITOR to buy a group of films, some which the exhibitor may not have wanted otherwise, in order to be guaranteed a few, high-quality or potentially high-revenue producing films.

BLOCKING
Laying out the ACTION or movement in a SCENE with the actors and/or camera.

BLOOM
Treatment of any glass surface, excluding the camera lens, with a special transparent fluoride coating to reduce glare. *See also DULLING SPRAY.*

BLOOP
1) A clicking noise caused when a faulty SOUND TRACK SPLICE passes through the reproduction equipment. This happens sometimes when the SPLICER becomes magnetized and puts a magnetic charge on the film. 2) The opaque, triangular patch applied to the splicing area, or painted on with blooping ink to silence that noise. The blooping ink can also be used to black out any unwanted areas on the film. This is called either blooping or de-blooping.

BLOOPER
1) SPECIAL EFFECTS device, usually a round open tank, used to simulate water explosions. 2) A missed line, CUE, etc., which is usually funny.

BLOW-UP
Enlargement by OPTICAL PRINTING. In the movies, this is usually done from 16mm to 35mm. Individual SHOTS may be blown up to be inserted in a film *(e.g., STOCK FOOTAGE shot in 16mm needed for a particular SEQUENCE).* The GRAIN, however, will be slightly different in the two shots. The opposite of a blow-up is a REDUCTION PRINT.

BLUE PAGES
Added pages and changes that are put into an already numbered SCRIPT once the scripts have been distributed on a PRODUCTION.

They are printed on colored paper, first blue, then pink, etc. with the date of the correction on the page. *See COLOR CODING.*

BLUE-SCREEN SHOT.
A delicate and elaborate SPECIAL EFFECTS process whereby the subject is filmed in front of a special, monochromatic blue BACKGROUND with normal film. Blue-sensitive MATTES are made to replace the blue background with other FOOTAGE. When combined, the subject and background look as if they were shot simultaneously. The bicycle flying scene in ET was shot in this manner. *See also CHROMA KEY, MATTE SHOT.*

'B' MOVIE *(aka B PICTURE)*
1) A term, originated in the old STUDIO days, used to describe a genre of movies shot on a low BUDGET, with a short PRODUCTION SCHEDULE, rarely using major STARS. Today, it is used loosely for about the same thing: EXPLOITATION or low budget films. 2) The second film in a DOUBLE FEATURE.

BNC
Abbreviation for Blimped Noiseless Camera, manufactured by the Mitchell Camera Co.

BO
Abbreviation for BOX OFFICE.

BODY FRAME/BODY BRACE
A device that secures a hand-held movie camera, such as a STEADICAM or PANAGLIDE, to the OPERATOR'S body during shooting.

BODY MAKE-UP ARTIST
According to UNION rules, a MAKE-UP ARTIST may only apply make-up from the top of an actor's head to the breastbone, and from the tips of the fingers to the elbow. Everything else falls under the jurisdiction of the Body Make-Up Artist.

BOFFO
A Hollywood TRADE PAPER slang term meaning big, terrific, extraordinary when referring to BOXOFFICE earnings, as in the hypothetical headline:
> *GHOSTBUSTERS...BOFFO BO!!!*

BOMB
The opposite of a HIT.

BOOM
A counter-balanced extension device which allows a camera or microphone to follow the ACTION in a fluid, continuous movement.

BOOM OPERATOR
A sound crew member who handles the microphone boom.

BOOM SHOT *(aka CRANE SHOT)*
A continuous shot incorporating a number of different CAMERA ANGLES from different levels, usually accomplished with the use of a crane.

BOOSTER
A device that increases the voltage of FLOODLAMPS to increase their output, and therefore their intensity.

BOOSTER LIGHT
Usually an ARC that illuminates shadowy areas. It improves detail, especially in Exterior Day shots.

BOUNCE BOARD
See REFLECTOR.

BOX OFFICE *(Abbr. BO)*
1) The place at a theater where one buys tickets. 2) Revenue generated by sales of tickets for admission to a film. 3) Slang term meaning an attractive, moneymaker, or a proposed project which has all the qualities of a potential moneymaker *(e.g., Robert Redford is considered good BOX OFFICE.)*

BOX RENTAL *(aka KIT RENTAL)*
A daily or weekly sum paid to a crew member for the use of his or her personal property *(e.g., make-up or hair dressing supplies, special tools)* during PRODUCTION.

'B' PICTURE
See 'B' MOVIE, 'A' PICTURE.

BREAKAGE
Additional monies paid by the NETWORK to a PRODUCTION COMPANY for the services of an actor. They are paying more money for said actor and are going over budget: *breaking* the budget in that area.

BREAK A LEG
Theatrical slang for *good luck*. It was derived from a superstition that it is bad luck to wish someone good luck, so the worst possible thing is wished to avoid any jinx. In French, people say *merde* instead of *break a leg*.

BREAKAWAY
PROPS that are specially designed to fall apart on impact, such as bottles, chairs, windows, etc. Used in STUNTS.

BREAKDOWN *(aka SCRIPT BREAKDOWN)*
1) When prepared by the PRODUCTION MANAGER or ASSISTANT DIRECTOR, it is an extremely detailed system of separating each and every element in the script and then re-arranging them in the most efficient and least expensive manner for filming. 2) A detailed analysis prepared by the SCRIPT SUPERVISOR for TIMING the SCRIPT. 3) To separate individual SHOTS from the DAILIES in the early stages of EDITING.

BREAKDOWN BOARD
See PRODUCTION STRIP BOARD.

BREAKEVEN
A highly subjective term used to identify a specific point at which monies generated by a film in release equal monies spent to create, DISTRIBUTE, and advertise that film, and that those people entitled to PROFITS may now start receiving them. Sometimes an ARTIFICIAL BREAKEVEN point can be established at a mutually-agreed income level that can be higher or lower than actual breakeven. Many times, the definition of breakeven varies from profit participant to profit participant within the same film, depending on what sort of deals were made UP-FRONT.

BREATHING
Rapid FOCUS fluctuations caused by film fluttering in the camera GATE.

BROAD *(aka BROADSIDE)*
A relatively large floor light used to increase the illumination of a large area without interfering with the MODELING lights. A single broad lamp uses a 500-750 watt lamp. A double uses two 1000-watt lamps.

BRUTE
The largest lighting unit on a SET. It is a high intensity carbon ARC spotlight with a 48 inch diameter LENS and uses 225 amps.

BUCKLE
When the film accidentally piles up in the camera or PROJECTOR because the LOOP is lost. The camera or projector cannot continue operating until this situation has been remedied.

BUDGET
An attempt to list every possible expense in the making of a film before the film is made. Accurate budgets can only be created after completely BREAKING DOWN a SCRIPT and preparing a PRODUCTION STRIP BOARD. It is usually prepared by the PRODUCTION MANAGER and also, for STUDIO pictures, by the studio Estimating Department. It is not unusual to have many budgets prepared during the course of PRODUCTION as more information is supplied, or as extenuating circumstances occur.

BUDGET FORM
A detailed list separated into categories of all the elements needed to make a film, how long they will be needed and how much they will cost. *See also ABOVE THE LINE, BELOW THE LINE and SCHEDULING.*

BURN-IN
To lay white TITLES, usually captions or SUBTITLES, over the picture in order to identify a person, place or thing, or to translate DIALOGUE.

BURNT-UP *(aka BLEACHED OUT)*
OVEREXPOSED film.

BUSINESS
1) Any small movement or action used by an actor in a SCENE to further the action and/or add color to the interpretation of his or her character *(e.g., Captain Queeg and his marbles in THE CAINE MUTINY, George Raft flipping his silver dollar, which became one of his trademarks).* 2) Referring to the motion picture industry in general, as in: *"he works in the business."*

BUS TO
As opposed to REPORT TO, this signifies a LOCATION DAY for the CREW. Their work (pay) time begins with the bus ride to the location and ends when they are dropped off after the completion of

the day's work. GOLDEN TIME does not begin until after 14 hours, as opposed to beginning after 12 hours of work in the STUDIO.

BUTTERFLY *(aka SILK)*
A device used to diffuse bright sunlight and harsh shadows when shooting.

BUTTON
A television term for a dramatic or comedic punch or topper at the end of a SCENE.

BUTT SPLICE
See SPLICE, TAPE SPLICE.

BUYER
1) A member of the PROP or WARDROBE department who finds, buys and/or rents the required equipment or wardrobe for a film. 2) A film buyer is a representative of a theater or theater chain who decides (recommends) which films to book.

BUZZ TRACK
A SOUND TRACK that carries a non-distinct BACK-GROUND noise and helps the EDITOR bridge the gaps in DIALOGUE which, otherwise, might sound unnatural. *See AMBIENCE, WALLAH.*

B/W
Abbreviation for Black and White.

B-WIND
Film that is used in the camera, wound so that it reads through the BASE, EMULSION side up, and in alternate GENERATIONS when printing. *See WIND, A-WIND.*

C

CABLE

1) Insulated wires that conduct electricity from a power source to equipment, generally available in 25-, 50- or 100-foot lengths. 2) Subscription television programming that is transmitted by cable to homes, schools, hotels, etc. The spectacular growth of the cable industry in the past few years has led to the development of programs and movies made specifically for cable.

CABLE PULLER *(aka CABLEMAN)*

The member of the SOUND CREW who handles the sound hookups, managing the many cables and wires to protect them from damage, and the CREW from injury.

CABLE RUN

The path of the cables from the power source (usually a GENERATOR) to the equipment being powered. This distance becomes important on LOCATION shooting where sources of power are scarce.

CALIBRATION

The process of measuring and marking FOCUS SETTINGS and F-STOPS on the LENS. While shooting, the FIRST ASSISTANT CAMERAMAN *(aka Technician)* usually adjusts the lens to pre-set focus stops, allowing the CAMERA OPERATOR to concentrate on composition and camera movement.

CALL
The time and location for the next day's (or night's) shooting. *See CALL SHEET.*

CALLBACK
1) An invitation for an actor to AUDITION again, once the field of competition has been narrowed, having successfully completed a prior audition. For SAG members there is a limit to the number of callbacks an actor may have before being paid for his/her time. 2) An automatic invitation to continue working as a DAY PLAYER unless specifically notified by the end of the day that he/she is laid off.

CALL SHEET
A list traditionally posted or handed out at the close of each shooting day. Prepared by the SECOND ASSISTANT DIRECTOR under the supervision of the FIRST ASSISTANT DIRECTOR and approved by the PRODUCTION MANAGER, the call sheet displays each cast and crew member's call times (REPORT TO the SET or to the spot for pre-arranged transportation to LOCATION), which SCENES to be shot, their order and which sets or locations will be utilized, COVER SETS, and any unusual equipment needed (CRANE, STEADICAM, etc.)

CAMEO
A small part played by a well-known actor or actress, usually to enhance the BOX OFFICE draw of a film.

CAMERA
A photographic device equipped with a LENS, a device (DIAPHRAGM) for regulating the amount of light which enters the camera through the opening (APERTURE), a movable screen (SHUTTER) which opens to let in light that EXPOSES the film, a VIEWFINDER (or through-the-lens viewing), a mechanism for advancing the film (or tape) and a lightproof housing (MAGAZINE) through which the film travels and is stored. The film is exposed to light in the housing of the camera.

CAMERA CAR
A specially-designed vehicle that carries the camera, its OPERATOR and usually the DIRECTOR, CAMERA ASSISTANT and other key personnel to film a moving vehicle or person.

CAMERA CREW
Consists of the DIRECTOR OF PHOTOGRAPHY, CAMERA OPERATOR, FIRST and SECOND ASSISTANTS, and a FILM LOADER.

CAMERA, HAND-HELD
A camera used by the OPERATOR not mounted on a TRIPOD. *See also STEADICAM, BODY FRAME.*

CAMERA JAM
When the PERFORATIONS of the film are not properly engaged in the SPROCKETS, or when the film is damaged, the film piles up on itself and jams, causing a BUCKLE. This can also occur in a PROJECTOR.

CAMERAMAN *(aka CINEMATOGRAPHER, DIRECTOR OF PHOTOGRAPHY)*
The person responsible for lighting the SCENE and, along with the DIRECTOR, setting up and composing SHOTS. A cameraman is usually chosen because of his/her lighting style and/or some particular specialty, such as shooting action, etc. The DP (known as DOP or Lighting Cameraman in England and Australia) is sometimes known as the First Cameraman, while the CAMERA OPERATOR is known as the Second Cameraman.

CAMERAMAN, ASSISTANT
See ASSISTANT CAMERAMAN.

CAMERA MOUNT
A device that allows the camera to be attached to a TRIPOD, DOLLY, CRANE, etc. *See also FRONT CAR MOUNT, SIDE CAR MOUNT.*

CAMERA MOVEMENT
The PANNING, TILTING or TRACKING of a motion picture camera. Good camera movement can add depth, drama and rhythm to a SCENE when used with sensitivity.

CAMERA OPERATOR *(aka SECOND CAMERAMAN)*
The member of the CAMERA CREW who runs the camera, taking instruction from the DIRECTOR and DIRECTOR OF PHOTO - GRAPHY. He is not responsible for creating the lighting or the style of movement, but is responsible for keeping the action IN FRAME, and to respond dramatically to the action as it happens, making ensuing camera movement look intentional.

CAMERA OPERATOR - HELICOPTER
Sometimes it is necessary to hire a camera operator who is specially trained in shooting motion pictures from helicopters. He will work closely with the helicopter pilot to get all the necessary SHOTS. *See also TYLER MOUNT, 'COPTER MOUNT.*

CAMERA REPORT
A detailed account prepared each day by the ASSISTANT CAMERAMAN listing the SCENES, the number of TAKES for each SHOT, the amount of film exposed and instructions as to the disposition of each take (PRINT, NG, etc.)

CAMERA TRACKS
Metal or wooden rails upon which the DOLLY rides during TRACKING (DOLLY) SHOTS.

CAN
1) A metal container for storing film. The term, *in the can,* refers to a completed film (or SCENE). 2) Headphones used by SOUNDMEN to monitor a recording. 3) A small, rectangular light that uses a 1000-watt lamp.

CANDELA *(Abbr. CD)*
The internationally recognized unit of measure for gauging the intensity of a light source.

CAPTION *(aka SUBTITLE)*
A line printed on the SCREEN to describe a SCENE, LOCATION or time. When captions are used to translate DIALOGUE into another language, they are referred to as subtitles.

CARBON ARC LAMPS
High intensity lamps and PROJECTOR bulbs whose light closely resembles sunlight. *See ARC.*

CARRY DAY *(aka HOLD)*
A day for which the cast and/or crew are paid, but not required to work.

CARTAGE
The term for reimbursement to a musician for the cost of transporting certain musical instruments to the STUDIO for MUSIC TRACK recording. If they are brought by public carrier, the PRODUCER pays the courier company directly.

28

CASSETTE
1) A lightproof container for film that allows a camera to be loaded in daylight. *See MAGAZINE.* 2) A container that houses audio or video tape, and protects the tape from damage.

CAST (n.)
Generally, the PERFORMERS appearing in a film. Specifically, on BUDGET and BREAKDOWN forms, cast refers only to SPEAKING PARTS, and not EXTRAS.

CAST (v.)
To choose the actors for a PRODUCTION. In a large BUDGET FEATURE FILM, there is usually a CASTING DIRECTOR and an EXTRA CASTING DIRECTOR. Very often, the casting of a film is done with BOX OFFICE considerations in mind.

CAST LIST
A compilation of actors'/characters' names, addresses, telephone numbers, agent contacts, listed either in alphabetical order, or according to how they are listed on the PRODUCTION BOARD. Usually, two separate lists are kept: one with confidential salary information for limited distribution among cast and crew (which must be submitted to SAG on all UNION pictures) and one without confidential information for general distribution.

CASTING DIRECTOR
The person (or company) responsible for interviewing, negotiating contracts with, and hiring most actors on a motion picture (television) project. He/she works under the supervision of the DIRECTOR and the PRODUCER.

CATWALK *(aka RIGGING or SCAFFOLDING)*
A suspended overhead structure or walkway on a SOUNDSTAGE that allows lighting and sound equipment to be hung high above the STUDIO floor.

CEL SIDE
The glossy, uncoated side of film that faces outward or inward on the roll, depending on the WIND. *See CELLULOID, A-WIND, B-WIND.*

CELLULOID
The trademark for a transparent BASE, coated on one side with light sensitive EMULSION. The uncoated, or CEL SIDE, on the film is

glossy, while the emulsion side is dull, and usually faces the center of the roll for camera STOCK. This base is highly flammable and has been replaced by the safer ACETATE *(aka SAFETY)* BASE.

CEMENT
Liquid adhesive used to SPLICE two pieces of film in HOT (or CHEMICAL) SPLICES.

CEMENT SPLICE
See SPLICE, HOT SPLICE.

CENTURY STAND *(aka C STAND)*
A small, three-legged stand with clamps. It can hold a GOBO, or small lights, for example.

CHANGE-OVER
The process of switching back and forth between two PROJECTORS at the end of each REEL so that the projection of a film will continue uninterrupted.

CHANGING BAG
A lightproof bag in which the FILM LOADER or SECOND ASSISTANT CAMERAMAN may load film into the MAGAZINE in broad daylight.

CHARACTER
The person an actor is portraying in a PRODUCTION.

CHARACTER NUMBER
The number assigned to the CHARACTER on the PRODUCTION BOARD. Usually, the more SCENES an actor has, the lower the number. For example, the stars in a production usually have numbers one through five.

CHEAT
To change the position of actors or PROPS in a SCENE in relation to the BACKGROUND when switching CAMERA ANGLES. Sometimes, in order for a DIRECTOR to get a desired CLOSE UP of an actor, he/she will move actors, props and/or camera angles to slightly different positions than they had in the MASTER SHOT. An actor (or piece of furniture, etc.) is, in effect, *cheated* out of the shot.

CHECK PRINT
The COMPOSITE print sent by the LAB for approval to check the DUPE NEGATIVE. If okayed, RELEASE PRINTS will be STRUCK.

CHECK THE GATE
One of the functions of the FIRST ASSISTANT CAMERAMAN. By physically looking into the gate of the camera, he/she can verify that there is no build-up of EMULSION or other foreign matter that would hinder or prevent proper operation of the camera.

CHEMICAL FADE
A FADE made by dipping one end of the NEGATIVE into a chemical reducer or one end of a POSITIVE into a chemical intensifier making the SCENE progressively disappear. Chemical fades usually produce poorer quality than OPTICAL FADES, but are quicker. They are rarely used.

CHILD ACTOR
Any actor under the age of 18. There are strict rules governing the working hours and conditions, etc., of child actors. Usually a TEACHER or WELFARE WORKER will be required on the SET. It is best to check with the SCREEN ACTORS GUILD for the most current rules.

CHINA MARKER
A grease pencil used by EDITORS to mark on film. It is semi-permanent, though it can be rubbed off and does not scratch the film.

CHINESE DOLLY
A SHOT in which the camera is pulled on DOLLY TRACKS slanted away from the subject, and is combined with a SWEEPING PAN.

CHOREOGRAPHER *(aka DANCE DIRECTOR)*
The individual who creates and supervises the dancing for PRODUCTION NUMBERS in a PRODUCTION. The DIRECTOR then decides how the numbers will be shot.

CHROMA KEY
A video MATTING process used in television, similar to the BLUE SCREEN process in film. *See also MATTE SHOT.*

CHROMATIC ABERRATION
A distorted IMAGE resulting from the fact that not all light waves bend at the same angle when passing through a LENS. For example, blue rays bend more than red and would not strike the surface of the film at the correct spot. The resulting image would look soft, or out of FOCUS. This was often used on purpose in silent films for its softening effect. To correct this problem, at least two lenses must be used: the second compensating for the chromatic aberration of the first. *See APOCHROMATIC LENS.*

CINCH MARKS
Scratches on the surface of the film caused by pulling the loose end of the film while the REEL is stationary. *See also ABRASIONS.*

CINEMASCOPE *(Abbr. SCOPE)*
20th Century Fox's trade name for a WIDE SCREEN process based on an ANAMORPHIC system using specially designed LENSES to squeeze the IMAGE during SHOOTING, then un-squeeze it during PROJECTION. When photographed on 35mm film, the Cinemascope ASPECT RATIO is 1:2.35 as compared with the standard 1:1.85. When filmed on 70mm film, the aspect ratio is 1:2.2.

CINEMATIC *(aka FILMIC)*
Adaptable to, or lends itself to film rather than to the stage. Usually used to mean the opposite of theatrical or stagey, or as a compliment that a DIRECTOR has used the medium well.

CINEMATOGRAPHER
See DIRECTOR OF PHOTOGRAPHY.

CINEMATOGRAPHY
The art and science of motion picture photography.

CINEMOBILE
Created by Fouad Said and mainly used for LOCATION shooting, it is a vehicle capable of handling all the required equipment for a film crew of 50. Some Cinemobiles include dressing rooms and bathrooms. The vehicle's first major assignment was the *I SPY* series. The company was bought by Filmtrucks in 1982.

CINERAMA
A WIDE SCREEN process that originally used three cameras and three PROJECTORS to record and project a single IMAGE of approximately 165 degrees.

CINEX STRIPS *(aka WEDGES)*
A test strip provided by the LAB with the DAILIES to indicate the range of densities possible for that NEGATIVE, and to enable the CAMERAMAN to see the accuracy of the EXPOSURE.

CLAP STICKS *(aka CLAPPER, CLAPPER BOARD)*
The part of a SLATE that makes an audible clack, used before or after a TAKE to provide a SYNC CUE to the EDITOR for picture and sound. If the clap sticks are used at the end of the SHOT, they are usually held upside down, and called end slate, or end marker.

CLEARANCE
Permission, paid for or not, to use someone else's copyrighted material (a book, song, poem, etc.) or a LOCATION in a film, video or television show.

CLICK TRACK
A small loop of magnetic film on which audible clicks of a metronome are placed, to be used when recording or SCORING a musical number. The CONDUCTOR uses headphones to listen to the click track so the clicks will not be recorded. When shooting a musical number, the clicks are audible on the PLAYBACK so the performers can move easily and rhythmically into the number.

CLIP *(aka TRIM or CUT)*
A small section of film removed from a SHOT by the EDITOR. *See also FILM CLIP*.

CLOSED SET
A set in a STUDIO or on LOCATION that is not open to any visitors or persons not immediatly connected with the PRODUCTION. Sometimes when intimate scenes are to be shot, only a limited number of crew members will be allowed on the set.

CLOSE-UP *(Abbr. CU)*
A SHOT taken at a short range or through a TELEPHOTO LENS, showing a detail of a subject. An actor's head and shoulders would be a close-up of that actor.

COBWEB MAKER
A device used by the SPECIAL EFFECTS department that blows rubber cement into fine strands on a SET to simulate spider's webs.

CODE AND RATING ADMINISTRATION OF THE MOTION PICTURE ASSOCIATION OF AMERICA

The organization that classifies films' suitability for different audiences. They also rate TRAILERS. *See RATINGS, MPAA.*

CODE NUMBERS

Small numbers put on the edge of picture and SOUND TRACKS with an encoding machine. Code numbers facilitate keeping picture and sound IN SYNC while CUTTING.

COLOR BARS

A chart containing strips of color covering the color spectrum, placed side by side and used by the LAB to check accuracy of reproduction of colors in processed film.

COLOR CODING

1) A system used when BREAKING DOWN a SCREENPLAY in order to create a PRODUCTION BOARD. Individual items in the screenplay (Cast, Props, Locations, etc.) are marked with different colors and then transferred onto BREAKDOWN SHEETS. A second color-coding system is used on the PRODUCTION BOARD to differentiate interiors from exteriors, day from night, etc. 2) A system standard in the industry for designating later versions (revisions) of a script or script pages. The color sequence is as follows: White, Blue, Pink, Yellow, Green, and Goldenrod.

COLOR CORRECTION

To change or alter specific color values during shooting by means of FILTERS, or during processing in the LAB.

COLOR REVERSAL INTERNEGATIVE

See CRI.

COLOR TIMER

The person at the LAB who corrects and/or balances the film to achieve correct color relationships and values. He frequently works with the DIRECTOR OF PHOTOGRAPHY to get the desired effects. *See TIMING.*

COMBINED PRINT

See COMPOSITE PRINT

COMMISSARY

The on-LOT restaurant in a STUDIO.

COMPLETION BOND
See COMPLETION GUARANTEE.

COMPLETION GUARANTEE
A contractual understanding that a motion picture will be completed and delivered in accordance with certain specifications, usually time, cost and conformity to SCREENPLAY, and sometimes in accordance with specifications of creative elements. It usually provides that the GUARANTOR will furnish monies to pay costs over BUDGET and CONTINGENCY and, in many instances, gives the guarantor power to take over control of the PRODUCTION if it appears to be out of control *(i.e., over budget and over schedule).*

COMPLETION GUARANTOR
See COMPLETION GUARANTEE.

COMPOSER
The person who writes the music for a film SCORE. Good film composers have the rare quality of being able to augment and enhance the visual elements of a film. A good score can make up for less than wonderful moments on the SCREEN.

COMPOSITE DUPE NEGATIVE
A duplicate negative that has both picture and sound IN SYNC on the same piece of film. *(See also DUPE NEGATIVE.)*

COMPOSITE MASTER POSITIVE
A FINE GRAIN positive PRINT combining picture and sound from which DUPE NEGATIVES can be made.

COMPOSITE PRINT
A positive print that has both picture and sound on one piece of film.

COMP/COMPS
Abbreviation for complimentary, and usually refers to free passes to a film or show.

COMPUTER GRAPHICS
Electronically generated IMAGES used in film and tape to create SETS, SCENES, etc. that are too difficult and/or too costly to build and shoot. Parts of the motion picture *TRON* were done with computer graphics.

CONDUCTOR
The person who interprets the SCORE and directs the orchestra. Often the COMPOSER conducts his/her own music.

CONE LIGHTS
Cone-shaped FLOODS that cover a large area with diffused, soft light. They come in SENIOR, JUNIOR and BABY sizes.

CONFORMING
Matching one piece of film to another *(e.g., conforming ORIGINAL NEGATIVE to cut WORK PRINT). See also NEGATIVE CUTTING.*

CONSTRUCTION CREW
Crew members who, under the supervision of the Construction Foreman, perform the tasks necessary to complete the SETS in and out of the STUDIO. The crew is made up of PROP MAKERS and LABORERS.

CONSOLE
The control panel used in a SOUND STUDIO for recording, re-recording, MIXING, etc.

CONSOLE DIMMER
A device used for light changes.

CONTACT LIST
A compilation of the names, addresses and telephone numbers of all the vendors, supply houses, services, etc. that will be used by a motion picture company during PRODUCTION. This list is constantly updated with new information.

CONTACT PRINT
A POSITIVE or NEGATIVE made by placing one piece of film in physical contact with another piece of unexposed film, then exposing the duplicate, FRAME by frame on a PRINTER in the LAB.

CONTACT PRINTER
See PRINTER.

CONTINGENCY
A certain amount of money, usually ten percent of the total NEGATIVE COST, that is included in the BUDGET to cover unexpected expenditures. Usually a COMPLETION GUARANTEE

will not be approved by the COMPLETION GUARANTOR unless a contingency is included in the final budget.

CONTINUITY
The orderly progression on ACTION from SHOT to shot for proper development of the story in a film. During shooting, the SCRIPT SUPERVISOR keeps track of SCENE details so there are no lapses in the continuity of DIALOGUE, action, SET DRESSING, PROPS or WARDROBE.

CONTINUITY PERSON
See SCRIPT SUPERVISOR.

CONTRACTOR
See MUSIC CONTRACTOR.

COOKIE
See KOOK.

COOPS
See BANK/COOP.

'COPTER MOUNT
A camera platform that is attached to a helicopter. It allows manned filming from the helicopter *(e.g., TYLER MOUNT)*.

COPY
See DUB, TRANSFER.

COPYIST
The person who extracts the parts for individual instruments from the SCORE for use by musicians and CONDUCTOR.

CORDLESS SYNC *(aka CABLELESS SYNC)*
An audio tape recorder that does not need a SYNC PULSE cable to remain IN SYNC with the camera, but used a CRYSTAL MOTOR whose speed is maintained by an accurate frequency signal from a vibrating crystal. The camera is governed by the same kind of crystal. *See NAGRA.*

CORE
The plastic spool that is used to store and hold film and RAW STOCK. NEGATIVES are usually stored on cores rather than REELS.

COST TO COMPLETE
The amount of money required, according to the BUDGET, to finish a picture. The financial status of the PRODUCTION is reported weekly on COST REPORTS.

COST REPORT
A detailed weekly analysis that identifies COSTS TO DATE, Costs This Week, and estimates the COST TO COMPLETE the film.

COSTS TO DATE
The amount of money per BUDGET category that has been spent on a PRODUCTION to date. *See COST REPORT, COST TO COMPLETE.*

COSTUME DESIGNER
The person who conceives and draws designs for the costumes (clothes) worn by the CAST on a PRODUCTION. He/she contributes to the overall *look* of the film as well as the interpretation of the character portrayed in the film.

COSTUMER
The person responsible for taking care of the COSTUMES on the SET or on LOCATION during PRODUCTION. On television shows that don't have COSTUME DESIGNERS, the WARDROBE SUPERVISOR is responsible for acquiring the clothes worn by the CAST. This is a UNION category separate from costumer. The old-fashioned term for costumer was Wardrobe Mistress.

COVERAGE
1) Shooting a SCENE from different CAMERA ANGLES so that the same ACTION is seen from different POINTS OF VIEW. These SHOTS are carefully EDITED to accomplish the dramatic objectives of the DIRECTOR - to create a SCENE that has movement, rhythm and drama. Coverage is made to accomplish the director's vision of a scene (how the scene will be seen). It accents performances, physical movement, rhythmic considerations of the scene, dramatic action, AMBIENCE (environment) etc. 2) The brief synopsis of story line and content of a project submitted for consideration, prepared by a STORY ANALYST. Usually the coverage includes a recommendation for any further action on the project.

COVER SET
An alternate SET that can be used quickly when circumstances (weather, illness, etc.) prevent shooting what was originally scheduled for that day. *See also BACK UP SCHEDULE.*

COVER SHOT *(aka INSURANCE TAKE)*
An additional printed TAKE which can be used in the event the preferred take is unusable *(e.g., damaged film)*.

CRAB DOLLY
Small, compact platform with wheels on which a camera is mounted for complex SHOTS. It can move easily in any direction.

CRADLE
A LENS support for extremely heavy and cumbersome lenses.

CRAFT SERVICE
The department of a film CREW that is responsible for the coffee, beverages and snacks on a SET. They also sweep up and do small chores. This is a UNION position on the West Coast.

CRANE *(aka WHIRLY)*
A large hydraulic lift for high ANGLE moving SHOTS, capable of carrying a camera and two people - usually the CAMERA OPERATOR and DIRECTOR or CAMERA ASSISTANT. It is one of the most complex pieces of equipment on a SET.

CRAWL
Rolling TITLES, usually used for END CREDITS, that begin at the bottom of the SCREEN and roll continuously to the top. Very rarely does one see rolling FRONT CREDITS.

CREATIVE DIFFERENCES
(aka ARTISTIC DIFFERENCES)
When two *creative* people (PRODUCER and DIRECTOR, director and actor, etc.) have ideas that are at such odds they find it impossible to work together. Often in the film business when a key member of the CAST or CREW is fired, "creative differences" is the reason cited.

CREDITS
1) The list of names and titles of the people who worked on the film. The size and placement of these credits in the FRONT CREDITS is an item negotiated for above the line personnel as well as some below the line personnel *(e.g., Production Designer, Costume Designer)*. Most union and guild contracts have very specific clauses governing the size and placement of their members' names in the END CREDITS. 2) Resumé of work history.

CREW
Those men and women who do all the technical and PRODUCTION jobs behind the camera to make a motion picture, video or television show.

CREW CALL
See CALL, CALL SHEET.

CRI
Abbreviation for COLOR REVERSAL INTERMEDIATE, more specifically COLOR REVERSAL INTERNEGATIVE. This is a NEGATIVE made directly from the original negative, using REVERSAL FILM STOCK, used when making RELEASE PRINTS. When using a CRI, the progression of GENERATIONS is: ORIGINAL (negative) to CRI to release print. In an alternate method, using an INTERPOSITIVE *(aka IP, PROTECTION MASTER, MASTER)* the progression is: original to IP to INTERNEGATIVE (called IP/IN) to release print. Because an extra step is involved, IP's are more expensive than CRI's. However, most LABS prefer IP's since CRI's have a tendency to streak. Also, the overall quality of the IP/IN is superior, and the GRAIN is finer. (Usually the more generations involved, the larger the grain. IP/IN, however, is considered to be one generation, not two.) Intermediate stages are used between negative and print to protect the original negative as much as possible. If an IP or CRI gets scratched, a new one can be made so ensuing release prints will be clean. It is always important to protect the negative.

CROP
To cut off, eliminate from FRAME.

CROSS-COLLATERALIZE
A controversial practice employed by the international DISTRIBUTION arms of the MAJOR STUDIOS whereby PROFITS and losses of EXHIBITING a picture (or pictures) in foreign countries are lumped together so that losses might wipe out any profits, and successes would, therefore, pay for failures. Although the accounting report is simpler for the PRODUCER (one statement instead of individual ones per country) this is a practice that clearly benefits the DISTRIBUTOR. On a smaller scale, the individual accounts on a project can be cross-collateralized so that the resulting final figures may be favorable (on or under BUDGET) even though there may have been OVERAGES in certain categories.

CROSS CUT
See INTERCUT.

CROSS-FADE
The gradual and simultaneous muting of one sound, while increasing another.

CROSS-PLOT
See PRODUCTION STRIP BOARD.

CRYSTAL SYNC
An electric device whose speed is adjusted by a vibrating crystal that emits a constant frequency signal. Used in sound recorders and cameras instead of a SYNC PULSE. *See CORDLESS SYNC, NAGRA.*

CS
Abbreviation for CLOSE SHOT.

CU
Abbreviation for CLOSE UP.

CUE
A pre-arranged signal for someone (actor, camera, EFFECTS, etc.) to perform a specific action.

CUCALORIS/KUKALORIS
See KOOK.

CUE CARDS *(aka SHOW CARDS, IDIOT CARDS)*
Large, lightweight cardboard signs on which the actor's lines are written. They are used mostly in television and are held right beside the camera so the actor can read them and make it look like he/she is speaking memorized lines. A newer, more accurate electronic device (TELEPROMPTER) is gradually replacing cue cards.

CUE MARK
A circle in the upper right hand corner of the FRAME in a film placed several feet before the end of the REEL to alert the PROJECTIONIST the next CHANGEOVER is approaching. They usually come in sets of two cue marks several seconds apart.

CUE SHEET
A list of DIALOGUE, music and EFFECTS cues in sequence as they appear in the SOUND TRACKS, used during the MIX. *See also MUSIC CUE SHEET.*

CUT
1) To change SCENES (SHOTS) without using any OPTICAL EFFECTS (WIPE, FADE, DISSOLVE, etc.). 2) A version of the completed film. *See DIRECTOR'S CUT, FINAL CUT.* 3) To eliminate material from the film or SCREENPLAY, etc.

CUT!
What the DIRECTOR says when he/she wants the film and sound and ACTION to stop.

CUTAWAY
An EDITING term describing when one CUTS from one SHOT to another in order to return to the first shot at a later point in the ACTION.

CUT BACK
An EDITING term describing when one returns to a SHOT after having CUT AWAY from it.

CUTTER
Another term for EDITOR.

CUTTER, NEGATIVE
The person who CONFORMS the NEGATIVE to the finished WORK PRINT and sometimes SPLICES it. Splicing, however, is often done by an assistant.

CUTTING *(aka EDITING)*
The art and science of editing the picture and SOUND TRACKS so that they form a logical, rhythmical progression that tells a story, sets a mood, etc. *See MONTAGE, EDITOR.*

CUTTING, NEGATIVE
The process of matching and cutting the NEGATIVE, FRAME for frame, to the FINAL CUT of the WORK PRINT. *See CONFORMING.*

CUTTING ROOM *(aka EDITING ROOM)*
A room equipped with EDITING equipment (KEM, MOVIOLA, BINS, CORES, SPLICERS etc.) ,where the EDITOR and assistants put the film together.

CYAN
One of the three PRIMARY COLORS used in color film, sensitive to one of the COMPLEMENTARY COLORS of light. Cyan (blue-green) reacts to red light, YELLOW to blue light and MAGENTA to green light.

CYCLORAMA *(aka LIMBO SET, CYC)*
A smooth, seamless BACKDROP or BACKGROUND on a SET.

D

DAILIES *(aka RUSHES)*
Usually, SCENES shot one day are rush processed and delivered by the LAB for viewing the next day by the DIRECTOR, PRODUCER, CINEMATOGRAPHER, EDITOR, etc., hence the name *dailies* or *rushes*. It should be noted that a SET should not be STRUCK until the dailies have been approved.

DANCE DIRECTOR
See CHOREOGRAPHER.

DAWN

The time of day when light begins to appear in the sky. This indicates a specific look, with pale colors, long shadows, etc. If dawn is indicated in a SCRIPT, it is important that it also be indicated on the BREAKDOWN SHEET. *(See MAGIC HOUR.)*

DAY

Indication in a SCRIPT and on BREAKDOWN SHEETS that the SCENE is to take place during daylight hours. If DAWN or DUSK is specifically needed, it generally is indicated and should be noted on the breakdown sheet.

DAY FOR NIGHT

A filming technique that, through the use of special blue FILTERS, allows exterior night SHOTS to be shot during the day. It is a technique devised in Hollywood, and is called, in French, *La Nuite Americaine*.

DAYLIGHT

The amount of measurable light combining both skylight and sunlight.

DAY OUT OF DAYS

A schedule showing the dates and times an actor will work.

DAY PLAYER

An actor hired by the day who has only a few lines or SCENES. According to SAG rules, Day Players must be personally notified before the end of the day's work that they are laid off, otherwise they will automatically be CALLED BACK. *See GUARANTEE.*

DAY SHOTS

Those SCENES in the PRODUCTION that are to be shot in daylight, either real or artificial, interior or exterior.

DEAL

A Hollywood term for an agreement, usually one that is legally binding, like a contract *(e.g., someone has a three-picture deal with Fox.)*

DEAL BREAKER

A point of concern in contract negotiations that, if not agreed upon, will mean the unsuccessful termination of the negotiations.

DEAL MEMO
A short written statement outlining the terms of an agreement in plain English. Until formal contracts are drawn and signed, deal memos are fully binding to all parties.

DECIBEL *(Abbr. DB or db)*
A unit of measurement of the intensity of sound waves.

DEFERRED COSTS/DEFERMENTS
Those expenses for which payment is postponed to a more convenient time. Or, payments which, by agreement, are contingent upon a film generating a certain negotiated level of income.

DEFINITION
Sharpness of FOCUS; the clarity of a photographed IMAGE.

DELETED PAGE
When a page is to be omitted from an already numbered SCRIPT, "page 24 omitted" is noted on the preceeding or subsequent page. This eliminates unnecessary, and confusing, re-numbering. *See also, ADDED PAGE, BLUE PAGES.*

DELETED SCENE
When a scene has been deleted or OMITTED, it is marked in the SCRIPT, "scene 124 omitted" to eliminate unnecessary and confusing re-numbering. *See also ADDED SCENE.*

DEPOLARIZER
A device that re-bends polarized light rays so that the object being photographed can be seen clearly through a piece of glass, or without harsh, reflected glare. For example, photographing a piece of art in a glass case, or framed behind glass, would require a depolarizer.

DEPTH OF FIELD
That distance from the camera in which an object stays IN FOCUS. Depth of field depends upon the focal length of the LENS, the APERTURE size and the distance of the object from the camera. The smaller the size of the aperture, the larger the number of the F-STOP and the greater the depth of field, and vice versa.

DESATURATED
To have certain colors taken out or eliminated from the film, either through the use of FILTERS over the LENS or by chemicals in the LAB. Certain film STOCKS lend themselves to desaturated color. One example of the use of desaturated color to achieve a

monochromatic effect in a film is the Dust Bowl sequence in Hal Ashby's *BOUND FOR GLORY.*

DEUCE
A SPOTLIGHT of 2000-watts, usually equipped with a FRESNEL LENS.

DEVELOP/DEVELOPMENT
1) To submit film to a chemical process (done in a LAB) that turns the LATENT IMAGE on the EXPOSED film into a visible image. 2) The preliminary stage in the process of making a motion picture that includes acquiring the literary rights, writing the SCREENPLAY, SCHEDULING, BUDGETING, SCOUTING the LOCATIONS, negotiating commitments of the DIRECTOR and principal CAST and, in INDEPENDENT PRODUCTIONS, raising money for PRODUCTION.

DEVELOPER
1) The chemicals used in the LAB that turn the LATENT IMAGE on EXPOSED film into a visible image. 2) The person who over - sees the aforementioned process.

DEVELOPMENT DEAL
An agreement between a STUDIO or PRODUCTION COMPANY and a PRODUCER or DIRECTOR or WRITER, to generate one or more film projects for eventual PRODUCTION.

DGA
Abbreviation for DIRECTORS GUILD OF AMERICA.

DIAGONAL SPLICING
A method of joining MAGNETIC FILM in which the film is cut on an angle to eliminate possible BLOOPS (or pops).

DIAL *(aka POT)*
A SOUNDMAN'S term for mechanically controlling sound during shooting and MIXING. To *dial out* or *pot it out* is to eliminate unwanted sound.

DIALOGUE
All spoken words.

DIALOGUE COACH/DIALOGUE DIRECTOR
A member of the CREW hired to assist the actors in learning their lines, or learning a particular accent.

DIALOGUE TRACK
The portion of the SOUND TRACK that carries the dialogue, as opposed to the MUSIC TRACK, the EFFECTS TRACK, etc.

DIAPHRAGM *(aka IRIS)*
A device that controls the amount of light passing through the LENS of a camera, PROJECTOR or PRINTER. It is usually made of overlapping metal leaves that form an opening (APERTURE) in the center. By adjusting the size of the opening (measured in F-STOPS), more or less light can be let in or out. *See also STOPPING DOWN, DEPTH OF FIELD.*

DICHROIC FILTERS
Gelatin or glass filters used on lamps to get rid of unwanted red light and to bring out more blue.

DIFFUSED LIGHT
Soft, gentle, shadowless light produced by placing DIFFUSERS over lights, or as a result of particles in the atmosphere, such as haze, fog.

DIFFUSER
Translucent material that is placed in front of lights in order to soften the harsh light hitting a subject.

DIGITAL EFFECTS
See COMPUTER GRAPHICS.

DIMMER
A rheostat that increases or decreases the amount of electricity reaching the object, usually a lamp.

DIN
Abbreviation for Deutsche Industrie Norm, the European system for measurement of a film's IMAGE gathering ability, or EMULSION SPEED. *See ASA, ISO.*

DINKY-INKY
Small, low wattage INCANDESCENT SPOT, usually 100 to 200-watts.

DIOPTER LENS
A lens placed in front of the normal camera lens for CLOSE UP photography with extremely sharp FOCUS.

DIORAMA
A miniature version of a SET.

DIRECTION
Instructions given by the DIRECTOR, or by the WRITER in the SCRIPT, or by the AD to the BACKGROUND, as to the ACTION, the mood, the rhythm of a SCENE, as well as how the scene is to be shot, etc.

DIRECTIONAL MIKE
In sound recording, the microphone that has a narrow angle of acceptance and picks up only selected areas.

DIRECTOR
The person ultimately responsible for all the creative aspects of a motion picture, theatrical or television show. He or she is hired by the PRODUCER, though some directors produce for themselves. *See also HYPHENATE.*

DIRECTOR, ASSISTANT
See FIRST and SECOND ASSISTANT DIRECTOR.

DIRECTOR OF PHOTOGRAPHY
(aka CAMERAMAN, CINEMATOGRAPHER)
The person responsible for LIGHTING (thus making a major contribution to the overall *look* of the film), FRAMING and SHOOTING a film, in collaboration with the DIRECTOR. He/she doesn't actually run the camera - that is the job of the CAMERA OPERATOR - but oversees everything having to do with camera and lighting.

DIRECTOR'S CUT *(aka FIRST CUT)*
The DIRECTOR'S version of the completed picture containing his audio and visual selections integrated into the completed picture. Under the DGA Basic Agreement, a film's director is entitled to the first cut of the film. *See also FINAL CUT.*

DIRECTORS GUILD OF AMERICA *(Abbr. DGA)*
The UNION for DIRECTORS, ASSISTANT DIRECTORS, PRODUCTION MANAGERS, etc., in America.

DIRTY DUPE
A black and white, untimed reproduction of a WORKPRINT. *See also ONE LIGHT PRINT.*

DISBURSING AGENT
The person in the accounting department who is in charge of paying out funds in a film, with the authorization of the financing entity or STUDIO.

DISSOLVE
An OPTICAL EFFECT that overlays the end of one SCENE with the beginning of another scene, so that simultaneously the first scene FADES OUT as the second scene FADES IN. Some cameras are equipped with dissolve controls, but most are done by an OPTICAL HOUSE or in a LAB. *See also A AND B CUTTING.*

DISTRIBUTOR
A company responsible for coordinating all aspects of the RELEASE of a motion picture, including the development and execution of the advertising campaign, arranging for EXHIBITORS, STRIKING PRINTS, collecting revenues and then distributing such revenues to any and all PROFIT participants in accordance with their contracts. Theatrical DISTRIBUTION FEES paid to the distributor are based on a negotiated percentage of the RENTAL (not BOXOFFICE) revenue generated by the motion picture. Distributors can also be licensed to distribute a film in such non-theatrical markets as television, pay/CABLE television, videocasettes, in-flight, armed forces, schools, libraries .

Most MAJOR STUDIOS have in-house distribution companies that handle the distribution of their own produced films as well as those acquired through NEGATIVE PICK-UP. Distribution divisions contribute to PRODUCTION decisions as well. The track record of a particular film, or genre of films, will help to decide whether or not another film should be produced or acquired.

DISTRIBUTION FEES
The fee required by the DISTRIBUTOR for his services.

DITTY BAG
An ASSISTANT CAMERAMAN'S pouch that contains all small items that he/she might need during shooting.

DOCU/DRAMA
A theatrical re-creation of actual events using actors. Although some of the events may have been altered for dramatic purposes, an effort is usually made to try to stay as close as possible to what actually happened.

DOCUMENTARY
A film or videotape of actual events using real people, not actors.

DOLBY
A trade name for a noise-reducing system in sound recording and reproduction. Many theaters are now equipped with Dolby systems for better film sound reproduction, and the costs of Dolby should be included in the BUDGET under POST-PRODUCTION and DISTRIBUTION expenses. There have to be non-Dolby PRINTS STRUCK for theaters not equipped with Dolby systems. A competitive system known as Ultra-Stereo was recently developed and requires less expensive conversion for theater owners.

DOLLY
A movable, wheeled platform that holds the camera and its operator, for TRAVELING (or dolly) SHOTS. The dolly is operated by a DOLLY GRIP, a member of the GRIP department. *See CRAB DOLLY, WESTERN DOLLY, ELEMACK DOLLY.*

DOLLY GRIP
See GRIP.

DOLLY SHOT *(aka TRAVELING, TRACKING or TRUCKING SHOT)*
A shot in which the camera moves while shooting. Dolly in = move in, Dolly out = move away from. *See DOLLY.*

DOLLY TRACKS
Rails or planks upon which the DOLLY, carrying the camera and operator, moves smoothly toward, along side of, or away from the subject. *See DOLLY SHOT.*

DOMESTIC VERSION
The CUT of a film that is RELEASED theatrically in the United States, as opposed to the version (possibly altered) released overseas, or an EDITED version prepared for television . *See FOREIGN VERSION.*

DOPE SHEET *(aka CAMERA REPORT)*
1) A list of all TAKES of every SHOT made. 2) A FILM LIBRARY list of the contents of a REEL of film. On a reel comprised of FILM CLIPS, the dope sheet lists what is contained in the various shots or SCENES so the viewer doesn't have to run through the whole reel when looking for a specific shot.

DOT
A DIFFUSER consisting of a small, flat, circular plate that reduces the light on the central subject.

DOUBLE
A person who resembles (or is made to resemble) a particular actor, and performs in SCENES that do not require acting *(e.g., walking through a crowd in LONG SHOT, driving by a LOCATION in a car.) See also STUNT DOUBLE, PHOTO DOUBLE.*

DOUBLE BILL
See DOUBLE FEATURE.

DOUBLE EXPOSURE
Two different IMAGES recorded on the same piece of film. *See also SUPERIMPOSE.*

DOUBLE FEATURE
Two films that play in the same theater one after the other for the price of one admission. *See 'A' PICTURE, 'B' PICTURE.*

DOUBLE MOVE
A move away from a LOCATION and then back to it. Generally, this is an expensive way of shooting and should be avoided.

DOUBLE SYSTEM
The preferred way to record sound with film - by taping the sound on separate magnetic tape at the same time the action is recorded by the camera. In SINGLE SYSTEM, sound is recorded directly onto the film. Although more portable, the sound quality is poorer and EDITING options are limited.

DOUBLE SYSTEM PRINT
A WORK PRINT with separate picture and SOUND TRACKS. *See INTERLOCK.*

DOUBLE TIME
Payment at twice the basic hourly rate for work performed on Saturdays, Sundays or union recognized holidays. *See also GOLDEN TIME.*

DOUBLING
A musician playing more than one instrument during a recording session. Musicians receive additional fees for doubling.

DOWNSTAGE
The FOREGROUND closest to the camera, or, on a stage, closest to the audience.

DOWN TIME
The period lost when making necessary equipment repairs, LOCATION moves, make up adjustments, WARDROBE changes, etc., before shooting resumes.

DRAPES
Cloths used for decorating the SET or changing the acoustics of the room.

DRESS
To decorate or change the appearance of an item or place so that it can be used for shooting. For example, *"dress the SET"* means to put all furniture, PROPS, etc., on the set; *"dress the windows for night"* means to change the look of what we see through the windows so it will appear to be nighttime outside.

DRIVE ON *(aka GATE PASS)*
Permission left by someone who works at a STUDIO with the guard at the gate for an outsider to enter a studio LOT for the purpose of visiting someone who works there or has an office there.

DRESS REHEARSAL
Rehearsal in COSTUME. Mainly a theatrical term.

DROP AND PICK UP
A specific UNION rule applying to actors that states there must be at least 10 free days between the last day that an actor works and the time he next works on a PRODUCTION, otherwise he must be paid for all non-working days in between. This can be done once per actor per production.

DRY RUN
Full DRESS REHEARSAL, with all CAST and CREW in place, with the camera moving, but not running.

DUARC
A double ARC used for FILL LIGHT. Duarcs are not focusable, thus are not used too much anymore.

DUB *(aka MIX, LOOP)*
1) To combine the different SOUND TRACKS by MIXING to produce a master recording from which the final sound track is then made.   2) Replacing the DIALOGUE with another voice or into another language.   3) Video term meaning to copy or to make a copy.

DULLING SPRAY
A spray, usually aerosol, that leaves a matte finish on objects that might otherwise cause a FLARE or HOT SPOT on the film. *See also BLOOM.*

DUMMY
A life-size doll used to DOUBLE a real actor in an extremely dangerous, or potentially dangerous, SCENE *(e.g., a car explosion)*.

DUPE (n.)
A PRINT made from CUT WORK PRINT. Usually made in order to meet a deadline or to allow the EDITOR to sent one print to the NEGATIVE CUTTER for CONFORMING and one to the SOUND MIXER. Dupes can also be made from RELEASE PRINTS - that is how pirating is done. More legitimately, however, is duping LIBRARY FOOTAGE or a SCENE from an old film that (with permission) is to be used in a new film. Compilation films *(e.g., THAT'S ENTERTAINMENT)* are made that way when original NEGATIVE is not available.

DUPE (v.)
To copy a film or tape recording. For video, the term DUB is used.

DUPE NEGATIVE
A negative made from a FINE GRAIN MASTER POSITIVE or INTERPOSITIVE, used to STRIKE RELEASE PRINTS. *See also CRI.*

DUSK
Twilight. When indicated in a SCRIPT, it must also be so noted on the BREAKDOWN SHEETS. *See also DAWN.*

DUVATYNE
Black cloth that is used on FLAGS and GOBOS to shield light from a particular part of the SET.

DYNALENS
Similar to a BODY FRAME, but made for a CAMERA CAR or helicopter, it is a stabilizer for the LENS with a GYRO that helps keep the camera steady in bumpy situations while shooting.

E

ECHO CHAMBER
A special room constructed to amplify sound reverberation and repetition.

ECU
Abbreviation for Extreme CLOSE UP.

EDGE NUMBERS
See KEY NUMBERS.

EDITING
The process of selecting, arranging and assembling a film and its SOUND TRACK into a logical, rhythmical story progression. The stages of editing are: ROUGH CUT - the first logical ASSEMBLY of the chosen FOOTAGE, FINE CUT - a more finely hewn, worked over version, FINAL CUT - the version to which the NEGATIVE will be CONFORMED, from which RELEASE PRINTS will be

STRUCK. The editing process is more one of evolution than one of finite stages, however. *See also CUTTING, MONTAGE.*

EDITING BENCH
A table with shelves in the back for storing materials, plus REWINDS and a light well for viewing film.

EDITING ROOM
See CUTTING ROOM.

EDITING TABLE *(aka FLATBED)*
A specially-designed workbench for viewing, CUTTING, and SPLICING film. *See STEENBECK, KEM.*

EDITOR
The person responsible for EDITING the film. Many times, this job can entail as much creative input as the job of the DIRECTOR. A good editor can take banal FOOTAGE and, by artful CUTTING, INTERCUTTING and addition of a moving SOUNDTRACK, turn it into an exciting piece of film. It is not uncommon these days for an editor and ASSISTANT EDITOR to start working on a picture during PRE-PRODUCTION, begin assembling DAILIES during PRODUCTION, and if the picture is not too complicated, present a ROUGH CUT within four-to-six weeks after completion of PRINCIPAL PHOTOGRAPHY. *See also CUTTER.*

EFFECTS *(Abbr. FX)*
Refers to illusory techniques, such as DISSOLVES, WIPES, FADES, that are usually added during POST PRODUCTION.

EFFECTS BOX
See MATTE BOX.

EFFECTS FILTER
A glass or gelatin filter that changes natural light to produce the illusion of fog, for example.

EFFECTS TRACK *(abbr. FX TRACK)*
The separate channel onto which SOUND EFFECTS are recorded.

EIGHTY SIX
Turn off. Tear down. Get rid of. *See STRIKE, KILL.*

ELECTRICAL TRUCK
Specially designed vehicle that holds and carries all the necessary electrical equipment for the PRODUCTION. Oftentimes these trucks have built-in GENERATORS.

ELECTRICIAN
Under the supervision of the GAFFER, this crew member sets and adjusts the lights.

ELEMACK DOLLY *(aka SPIDER DOLLY)*
A small, light, extremely-maneuverable, wheeled platform introduced in this country from Italy in the 60s. It features long, adjustable legs and can fit easily through doorways.

ELEMENTS, LENS
The concave and convex pieces of precision ground glass that comprise a photographic lens.

ELR *(aka ADR)*
Abbreviation for Electronic Line Replacement. *See LOOPING.*

ELS
Abbreviation for Extreme Long Shot.

EMMY
The television equivalent to OSCAR, awarded annually by the Academy of Television Arts and Sciences. They are awarded both nationally and locally in various categories.

EMULSION
The light sensitive substance on film. It is dull and faces inward on the roll on B-WIND STOCK, which is used in the camera.

EMULSION NUMBER *(aka BATCH NUMBER)*
A code on RAW STOCK to indicate the particular batch of emulsion used to create that film stock.

EMULSION SPEED
The light gathering properties of a film's emulsion, indicated in ASA, ISO or DIN numbers. When shooting in low light, a film with a high emulsion speed is required, and conversely, as the light increases, a film with a lower emulsion speed is used. The selection of the proper film speed for a given situation is necessary for correct EXPOSURES. In controlled lighting situations, emulsion speed is a

factor because different emulsions give different visual qualities: saturated color, desaturated and rough GRAIN, etc.

END CREDITS

The list of CAST and CREW who worked on a motion picture. Size and placement of names on the SCREEN are usually contractual. Any other guaranteed credits, such as acknowledging special LOCATIONS, as well as IA and MPAA seals are usually placed at the end of these credits. Most end credits roll, as opposed to MAIN CREDITS (aka FRONT CREDITS) that appear one at a time in the beginning of the film.

END SLATE

The audio/visual mark given by the SECOND ASSISTANT CAMERAMAN to denote the end of the scene. The CLAPSTICKS are held upside down in front of the camera for a few seconds and then clacked together.

EPIC

A larger than life story *(e.g., DR. ZHIVAGO, EXODUS LAWRENCE OF ARABIA).*

EQUALIZER

A regulating device for shaping the frequency of sound waves to produce the desired sound.

EQUITY *(aka ACTORS EQUITY)*

The actors UNION for stage/theater. *See also SCREEN ACTORS GUILD.*

ESTABLISHED

1) Persons of objects that have been previously filmed or seen by the camera. 2) Known at Spago's.

ESTABLISHING SHOT

Usually a LONG or FULL SHOT at the beginning of a SEQUENCE to specify (ESTABLISH) the LOCATION, mood setting, etc.

EXCHANGE

Regional offices that are responsible for distributing motion pictures to theaters in their area.

EXCITER LAMP
Used in recording OPTICAL SOUND TRACKS and when PROJECTING sound films, this small, bright INCANDESCENT lamp shines light through the printed optical track on the film to activate the optical sound reader, which converts light waves into sound waves.

EXECUTIVE PRODUCER
The title usually given to the person responsible for either financing the film or securing the financing for the film. In some cases, the executive producer credit can be given to the UPM or some other person associated with the PRODUCTION. It can even be the star's AGENT.

EXPENDABLES
Those items that are purchased for use on a film that will probably be used up *(e.g., light bulbs, tape, GELS.)*

EXPLOITATION
Advertising, publicity, merchandising, licensing and pro-motion of a film.

EXPLOITATION FILM
A FEATURE FILM whose subject matter includes gratuitous sex, violence, etc., and little redeeming social value, and whose advertising /publicity *(aka EXPLOITATION)* campaign capitalizes on it.

EXPOSED FILM
Film that has been subjected to light, but not PROCESSED. *See also LATENT IMAGE.*

EXPOSURE
1) Subjecting film to light. 2) The F-STOP and film speed settings used to photograph a SCENE. *See also F-STOP, T-STOP, EMULSION SPEED.*

EXPOSURE METER *(aka LIGHT METER)*
A device that measures the intensity of light (direct or reflected.) The two basic types of exposure meters are: INCIDENT LIGHT METER, which measures the amount of light falling on a subject; and REFLECTED LIGHT METER, which measures the amount of light bouncing off the subject. For example, a subject dressed all in white against a white BACKGROUND would reflect more light than

a subject dressed in black against a dark background, even when lit with exactly the same amount of light. *See also PHOTOMETER.*

EXT.
Abbreviation for EXTERIOR.

EXTENSION TUBE
A LENS attachment that permits the lens to be positioned at a greater distance from the camera housing so as to facilitate CLOSE UP SHOTS.

EXTERIOR
Any SCENE shot out-of-doors.

EXTRA
An actor who speaks no lines (except as part of a group) and who makes no gesture to set him/her apart from the other extras. *See BACKGROUND, ATMOSPHERE, SILENT BIT, SCREEN EXTRAS GUILD.*

EXTREME LONG SHOT *(Abbr. ELS)*
A shot taken from some far-away high or low ANGLE, usually used as an ESTABLISHING SHOT.

EYE LINE
The ACTOR'S line of vision. Usually kept clear of people or objects that may distract him/her while working. Also an important factor in CONTINUITY - making sure the actor's eyes are looking in the same direction in the COVERAGE of a scene that they were in the MASTER SHOT.

F

FADE
An OPTICAL EFFECT that causes one SCENE to emerge or disappear slowly. Movies usually begin with a FADE IN and end with a FADE OUT. Until the 60s, it was common practice to begin and end SCENES with fades. These days most people use straight CUTS between scenes unless a specific EFFECT is desired, either for visual reasons, indications of passage of time, etc.

FADE IN/FADE UP
To go from black to a full picture over a certain time frame, usually a few seconds or so.

FADE OUT/FADE DOWN
The opposite of FADE IN, to go from picture to black gently over a few seconds.

FAST FILM
Film whose ASA is higher than 100, thereby allowing low-light SHOTS to be made.

FAST-MOTION
See ACCELERATED MOTION.

FAVORED NATIONS
A shorthand phrase used in negotiations and in informal contracts to denote that a party will be afforded treatment equal to the best given by the PRODUCER. Often used in defining the PROFITS for the participants (actors, DIRECTOR, etc.) the size and placement of BILLING or the calibre of dressing rooms, motor homes on the SET, etc.

FAVORING
The situation in which the camera (or microphone) is placed nearer to one actor than the others, resulting in an emphasis on that actor. *See also CHEAT.*

FEATURE (n.)
A full length film of at least 85 minutes.

FEATURE (v.)
To favor, give preferential treatment *(i.e., better BILLING).*

FEATURE LENGTH
A film usually 85 minutes long or more.

FEATURED PLAYERS
An unofficial term used to designate a PRINCIPAL PLAYER who does not have a starring role, but has higher BILLING and, usually, higher pay than a DAY PLAYER. Featured players are not main characters, but are still considered speaking cast parts and are treated as such on the BREAKDOWN SHEET and BUDGET.

FIELD OF VIEW
The angle covered by the camera LENS.

FILL
Wasted (NG) or blank film put into WORK PRINT during EDITING when a SCENE is missing to keep the film IN SYNC. Sound fill is usually FOOTAGE from discarded RELEASE PRINTS.

FILL LIGHT *(aka FILLER LIGHTS)*
Secondary lamps used to illuminate shadows and soften the harshness sometimes caused by the KEY LIGHT. *See LIGHTING.*

FILM
1) A movie. 2) ACETATE-based, EMULSION-coated strip with PERFORATIONS on the edges, used to make photographic IMAGES when exposed to light in a camera or projected through a PROJECTOR.

FILM ARCHIVE
A library of materials *(e.g., films, posters, aka ONE-SHEETS, magazines)* that relate to film. A place that stores and preserves collections of films where films may be viewed for research or other purposes.

FILM CLIP
A relatively short section of a film that is isolated and used for promotional or other purposes *(e.g., a compilation film like THAT'S ENTERTAINMENT)*.

FILMIC
A trendy Hollywood term meaning CINEMATIC.

FILM LEADER
A length of film, attached to the HEAD and TAIL of REELS of processed film by the LAB, that protects the film while it is being threaded onto, or wound off of, the PROJECTOR. *See also ACADEMY LEADER, UNIVERSAL LEADER.*

FILM LOADER
The CAMERA CREW member whose job it is to load and unload MAGAZINES, and keep the LOADING ROOM in ship shape condition.

FILM MAGAZINE *(aka MAGAZINE)*
A lightproof cassette for storing and holding film.

FILM STOCK/RAW STOCK
Unprocessed, unexposed film.

FILTER
A colored or clear plate of glass or gelatin, that, when placed over the camera or PRINTER LENS absorbs a particular part of the light spectrum, corrects for color imbalance, or diffuses the light. The most basic color filters are: 1) Daylight #85 - When used with a Neutral Density filter and high speed film, produces a crisp, bright, cheerful outdoor IMAGE. *See FAST FILM.* 2) Diffusion - Spreads the light, softens shadows and harsh lines. 3) Fog - Similar to a

diffusion filter except that it creates an illusion of fog. Available in varying degrees of greyness. 4) Neutral Density *(aka ND)* - Evenly reduces the amount of light reaching the film, thereby lowering the contrast and subduing (or DESATURATING) colors slightly. 5) Polarizing - To control glare or reflection. *See DEPOLARIZER.* 6) UV (ultraviolet, *aka SKY FILTER*) - Reduces the bluish cast caused by ultraviolet light on color film. Useful for higher altitudes to reduce distance haze. *See HAZE FILTER.* 7) Protection - An optical glass lens used to protect the camera lens from weather, dust, etc.

FILTER FACTOR
The amount by which EXPOSURE will have to be increased to compensate for the light absorbing qualities of a FILTER.

FINAL CUT
1) The finished version of the WORK PRINT to which the NEGATIVE is CONFORMED in order to STRIKE the RELEASE PRINTS that will be shown in theaters. 2) An important point when negotiating a DIRECTOR'S or PRODUCER'S contract to determine who has the last word on the form and content of the version that will be released. *See also WORK PRINT, DIRECTOR'S CUT.*

FINANCING
The monetary support for a film project. *See BANK.*

FINANCING ENTITY
The person or company that is paying for the PRODUCTION of a film.

FINANCING FEES
An amount of money paid to the FINANCING ENTITY and/or person who arranged for the FINANCING. *See EXECUTIVE PRODUCER.*

FINE CUT
A much more refined version of the WORK PRINT after the ROUGH CUT. *See also EDITING.*

FINE GRAIN
1) Refers to film EMULSION. 2) A black and white POSITIVE (like an INTERPOSITIVE) used mainly for producing the DUPE NEGATIVE, where clarity, not speed, is important.

FIRST ASSISTANT CAMERAMAN
A member of the camera crew who loads and unloads MAGAZINES (if there is no SECOND ASSISTANT CAMERAMAN), changes LENSES, keeps the camera in proper working condition, maintains FOCUS while the camera is in motion, fills out CAMERA REPORTS (if there is no Second Assistant Cameraman), MARKS the spots where the actors will stand, and takes the measurement between the object being photographed and the lens. On most PRODUCTIONS, there usually is a SECOND ASSISTANT CAMERAMAN.

FIRST ASSISTANT DIRECTOR
The DIRECTOR'S right hand (called a First AD) who is usually a member of the DIRECTORS GUILD OF AMERICA (DGA) or another Guilld or Unon outside the United States which covers production people. He/she is the liaison between the director and PRODUCTION MANAGER, and can sometimes double as the production manager on smaller PRODUCTIONS. During PRODUCTION, he/she is responsible for the EXTRAS, keeping the production moving, and for the CALL (making sure that everyone and everything is in the right place at the right time), maintaining order and discipline on the SET. He/she orders *"Quiet on the set!"* before a TAKE and tells the CAMERA OPERATOR to ROLL. Before production begins, the AD BREAKS DOWN the SCRIPT, determines the number of extras and SILENT BITS needed for each SCENE, and, with the director's and production manager's approval, hires them. The First AD usually has an assistant called a Second. *See also SECOND ASSISTANT DIRECTOR.*

FIRST CUT
See DIRECTOR'S CUT.

FIRST DOLLAR
A term used to indicate the first money that a motion picture generates in RELEASE. GROSS PROFIT participants and DISTRIBUTORS usually take their cuts from the first dollar, while NET PROFIT participants wait until the picture has BROKEN EVEN. *See ARTIFICIAL BREAKEVEN.*

FIRST DRAFT
The first complete version of a SCREENPLAY in CONTINUITY form including full DIALOGUE.

FIRST RUN
The first RELEASE of a motion picture in a major market area
*(e.g., in Los Angeles, selected theaters in Westwood and
Hollywood).*

FISHEYE LENS
Extremely WIDE ANGLE lens that causes a distorted IMAGE.

FISHPOLE
An extension rod on which microphones can be suspended. Used in
situations in which a BOOM would be too cumbersome.

FLACK
Slang for a publicity person, PRESS AGENT.

FLAG
A sheet of black material (DUVATYNE) that is set in a frame and
shades a particular part of a SET, an object or the camera from the
light. *See GOBO.*

FLANGE
Metal or plastic disc attached to a REWIND to facilitate the uniform
rewinding of the film in the CUTTING ROOM. *See also CORE.*

FLARE
Bright spot or flash on exposed film, usually from a reflection of a
shiny object. Can be avoided or eliminated by using DULLING
SPRAY. *See BLOOM.*

FLASH (n.)
A very short CUT or SEQUENCE that is used for dramatic effect.

FLASH (v.)
A means of increasing overall EXPOSURE (especially in shadow
areas) by briefly exposing unexposed and unprocessed film to light.
This process flattens contrast. It is a tricky procedure, usually done
by the LAB.

FLASHBACK
A jump backwards in chronological time for dramatic effect or
story/plot purposes.

FLASHFORWARD
A jump ahead in chronological time for dramatic effect or story/plot
purposes.

FLASH FRAMES
Overexposed film frames at the beginning of a SHOT that received too much light while the camera was reaching proper speed. Sometimes, in order to mark the beginning of a SCENE for the EDITOR, the CAMERAMAN will intentionally flash a few frames.

FLASH PAN *(aka SWISH or WHIP PAN)*
A rapid PAN (side to side movement of the camera rotating on TRIPOD) that produces an almost complete blur.

FLAT
1) An IMAGE with little or no contrast or DEPTH OF FIELD.
2) A large, movable section of a SET.

FLATBED
A motorized EDITING device, where REELS of film (sound and picture) run side to side during viewing (instead of upright, as on a MOVIOLA). This makes it possible to easily run several different TRACKS simultaneously with the picture. Two name-brands are STEENBECK and KEM.

FLAT PRINT
A standard print projected normally. The opposite is a squeezed print. *See ANAMORPHIC LENS, WIDE SCREEN.*

FLAT RATE
An unchanging fee paid for services rendered. This differs from a weekly or hourly rate in that no overtime is paid. A PRODUCER may attempt to negotiate a flat rate for an employee rather than worry about hourly wages, overtime, GOLDEN TIME, etc.

FLICKER
A bothersome occurrence when motion picture film is projected at a rate of fewer than 24 frames per second. *See PERSISTENCE OF VISION.*

FLOODLIGHT *(aka FLOOD)*
An extremely powerful lighting unit that illuminates a large area of the SET. Standard floods cannot be focused, while focusing floods can be.

FLOOR
The shooting area of a SOUND STAGE.

FLY
1) Heavy scenery on ropes (cables) above a SET. 2) Slang for "will this work?" *(e.g., "Do you think this deal will fly?")*

FOCAL LENGTH
The size of a LENS, indicated in millimeters. The smaller the focal length, the wider the angle of view, and vice versa.

FOCAL SETTINGS
Predetermined positions on the focusing ring on the LENS that allows the FOCUS PULLER *(aka TECHNICIAN, FIRST ASSISTANT CAMERAMAN)* to correctly maintain focus during difficult SHOTS. *See also FOLLOW FOCUS, FOLLOW SHOT.*

FOCUS (n.)
The point where rays of light refracted by a LENS converge.

FOCUS (v.)
To adjust the LENS to produce a crisp, sharp IMAGE.

FOCUS PULLER *(aka TECHNICIAN, FIRST ASSISTANT CAMERAMAN)*
A CAMERA CREW member whose job it is to measure the distance from the LENS to the subject with a tape measure and maintain focus while the camera is rolling. He/she is in charge of all cameras and other equipment as well as all the other assistants on the camera crew. *See ASSISTANT CAMERAMAN, FIRST and SECOND ASSISTANT CAMERAMAN.*

FOG
1) The density that results from inadvertently exposing film to light. 2) A visual EFFECT produced by machines to heighten ATMOSPHERE in a SCENE.

FOG FILTER
DIFFUSING filter placed on the camera LENS to create the effect of fog.

FOG MACHINE
A SPECIAL EFFECTS device that creates cool smoke that sits low on the ground to give the effect of fog or mist.

FOLEY
Any body movement sound or SOUND EFFECT that is recorded in a STUDIO as the picture for a SCENE is run, and is then CUT into

the film. For example, in a chase scene on foot, a FOLEY ARTIST would watch the scene to be foleyed and recreate the actions of the actor while creating believable sounds *(footsteps, panting, etc.)* . A punch might be created by slugging a piece of meat. In a MUSICAL, the sound of tap dancing would be recreated by the dancers on a FOLEY STAGE while watching the dance FOOTAGE. *See also STREAMER.*

FOLEY ARTIST
A specialist who is called upon to recreate certain body movements and other sounds. In television, the foley artist is sometimes a member of the EDITING staff.

FOLEY STAGE
One of several in a FOLEY STUDIO, these large rooms have various types of floor surfaces and other objects to create most of the SOUND EFFECTS needed for a picture.

FOLEY STUDIO
A specially designed recording studio that has facilities to project picture and sound simultaneously while recording new sounds which are being created by the FOLEY ARTIST(s). The SOUND Effects are recorded on FULL TRACK, usually three- or four-stripe, so as to give the EDITOR three attempts at getting the right sound. The sounds are then cut into the film IN SYNC.

FOLEY TRACKS
A 35mm copy of recorded foley sounds to be CUT and SYNCHED into the film by the EDITOR. The original FOLEY MASTER is stored for safekeeping until the completion of the film, when it will be MIXED into the final SOUNDTRACK.

FOLLOW FOCUS
Maintaining a sharp IMAGE during shooting, while TRACKING the movement of the subject. *See FOCUS PULLER, FIRST ASSISTANT CAMERAMAN.*

FOLLOW SHOT
A shot in which the camera TRACKS (or appears to follow) the subject, or goes where the subject goes. *See also PAN, TILT, TRACKING SHOT.*

FOOT *(aka TAIL)*
The end of the film (or tape) REEL.

FOOTAGE

Any length of film, expressed in feet and frames, rather than feet and inches. 16 frames = 1 foot of 35mm film. Can refer to any part of a film, from one shot to the entire film. At 24 frames per second (FPS), 1 foot plus 8 frames pass through the camera per second. Therefore, in 60 seconds, 90 feet of film have been exposed.

SECONDS	FEET		FRAME
1	1	+	8
2	3	+	0
3	4	+	8
4	6	+	0
5	7	+	8
10	15	+	0
30	45	+	0

FOOTAGE COUNTER

A gauge on the camera, PROJECTOR or PRINTER that measures the amount of film exposed, projected or printed, etc. Fractions of a foot are expressed in FRAMES not inches. *See FOOTAGE.*

FOOTCANDLE

A unit of illumination measured at a distance of one foot from the light source.

FORCED CALL

Violation of a UNION or GUILD contract by bringing a CREW or CAST member back to work before he or she has had the minimum amount of time off.

FOREGROUND

1) The part of the SET closest to the camera. 2) The part of the IMAGE closest to the front *(i.e., not in the BACKGROUND). See also DOWNSTAGE.*

FOREIGN DISTRIBUTION

The EXPLOITATION and sales of a motion picture in markets outside the United States and Canada theatrically, and the United States alone for television/cable and other non-theatrical markets. *See also CROSS-COLLATERALIZATION.*

FOREIGN SALES REP

The person or company authorized to sell RIGHTS and to EXPLOIT that film in foreign markets. Most foreign sales reps sell country by country, or market by market, and do not CROSS-COLLATERALIZE.

FOREIGN VERSION
A version of a film prepared for RELEASE in a language other than the original language of the film. Foreign versions are either SUBTITLED or DUBBED. The actual form of the film may be altered for foreign markets.

FORMAT
The width to height ratio of the film as it is projected on the SCREEN (*e.g., standard as opposed to WIDE SCREEN format.*) *See also ASPECT RATIO.*

FOUR-WALL
To rent a theater for a flat fee in order to EXHIBIT a motion picture. This practice is usually reserved for LOW-BUDGET, INDEPENDENT or art films that are looking for a DISTRIBUTOR or trying to find an audience. Four-walling can be repeated from town to town, hopefully generating good WORD-OF-MOUTH and REVENUE.

FPS
Abbreviation for FRAMES PER SECOND, and sometimes feet per second. *See also PERSISTENCE OF VISION.*

FRAME (n.)
The individual unit of measurement and division of a length of film. Each frame contains an IMAGE. When these images are projected in succession (24 frames per second) an illusion of normal movement is created. More or less frames per second create the illusion of SLOW andACCELERATED MOTION.

FRAME (v.)
1) To compose the IMAGE in a SHOT through the VIEWFINDER of the camera. 2) To line up the film in the PROJECTOR or EDITING machine GATE so the entire frame (image) is visible.

FRAME COUNTER
A device that is attached to a camera, projector or printer that keeps track of how many frames have been exposed or projected.

FRAME DOWN
The action taken by the PROJECTIONIST when the bottom of the picture is cut off the SCREEN. The GATE of the projector is moved

down to the bottom of the FRAME of the film. This centers the picture properly up on the screen.

FRAMES PER SECOND *(Abbr. FPS)*
The number of frames of film that pass through a camera, PROJECTOR or PRINTER in one second.

FRAME UP
To center the picture properly on the SCREEN by moving the GATE of the PROJECTOR up. The opposite of FRAME DOWN.

FREELANCE
To perform certain duties (PRODUCER, DIRECTOR, WRITER, GAFFER, BOOM MAN, etc.) and submitting invoices or time cards for services rendered instead of being under long term contract on staff to the company. *See INDEPENDENT CONTRACTOR.*

FREEZE FRAME
A SHOT in which one frame has been printed over and over, appearing as a still IMAGE on the screen. *See also DOUBLE PRINTING, SKIP FRAMING.*

FRESNEL LENS
Named after its inventor, Augustin Jean Fresnel, it is a large lens with a surface composed of many small lenses arranged to produce a short FOCAL LENGTH, used on search lights, SPOTLIGHTS, etc.

FRICTION HEAD
A TRIPOD attachment that allows smooth camera movement while PANNING or TILTING.

FRINGE BENEFITS
1) Additional compensation (usually not in cash) over and above salary. If the individual is a member of a GUILD or UNION, vacation pay, as well as health, welfare and pension benefits are paid to the organization of which that person is a member. 2) Free SCREENINGS for STUDIO employees, or a Christmas bonus from the boss, are some examples of fringe benefits a job might offer. *See also PERK.*

FRINGE RATES
Those wages in addition to direct wage compensation that are paid on behalf of an employee *(e.g., health and welfare, pension, taxes.)*

FRONT CAR MOUNT
A special device attached to the hood of a car that holds the camera. The action, either inside the car or out, can be shot while the car is driving or being towed. It is especially useful in STUNT driving shots.

FRONT CREDITS
The list, with emphasis on position, of the major contributors to the PRODUCTION of the film. Usually DISTRIBUTION COMPANY, PRODUCER or PRODUCTION COMPANY presents a (name of DIRECTOR) film, then the stars names, film title, ACTORS (in order of importance of role) CASTING DIRECTOR, COSTUME DESIGNER, COMPOSER, EDITOR, CINEMATOGRAPHER, PRODUCTION DESIGNER, SCREENWRITER, PRODUCER and, last, DIRECTOR.

FRONT PROJECTION
The opposite of REAR PROJECTION or BACK PROJECTION that can produce a brighter IMAGE. This is the system most commonly used in theaters.

FS
Abbreviation for FULL SHOT.

F-STOP
A number on the LENS that indicates the size of the APERTURE, which regulates how much light can enter the lens to expose the film. The f-stop is found by dividing the FOCAL LENGTH of the lens by the diameter of the aperture. *See also DEPTH OF FIELD, T-STOP.*

FULL COAT
Thirty-five millimeter film that is coated with magnetic ferrous-oxide. Usually PRODUCTION sound (recorded IN SYNC with the picture) is transferred onto full coat so it can be CUT in sync with the picture. Sound recorded in a FOLEY STUDIO or an ADR studio may be recorded directly onto full coat. There are usually four channels (or stripes) recorded on full coat, although there can be as many as six, as distinct from SINGLE STRIPE, which has one channel.

FULL SHOT *(Abbr. FS)*
A shot that includes the subject from head to toe, the main subject matter.

FX
Abbreviation of EFFECTS.

G

G
MPAA rating that means a film has been approved to be seen by all audiences. *See also RATING, MPAA.*

GAG
Slang for STUNT.

GAFFER
The chief electrician on the SET who is responsible for the lighting of the set according to the instructions of the DIRECTOR OF PHOTOGRAPHY. The gaffer supervises his electrical crew's place - ment of lights before and during shooting.

GAFFER'S TAPE *(aka DUCT TAPE, ELECTRICIAN'S TAPE)*
A wide, durable, silver cloth tape that will stick securely to most surfaces, but will not mar surfaces in good condition when removed.

GATE
The opening where the film is held in the camera while being exposed, in the projector while being projected, or the printer while

being printed. It can swing out, like a gate, for cleaning and threading.

GATE PASS
See DRIVE ON.

GAUGE
Refers to the width of the film.

GAUZE (aka CHEESECLOTH)
Thin, meshed cloth like the type used for bandages, often placed over a LENS to achieve a soft effect similar to a DIFFUSION FILTER.

GEARED HEAD
A complex camera support that fits onto a TRIPOD or DOLLY. It has gears and is wound to allow smooth PANS and TILTS of the camera - as opposed to a FRICTION HEAD, which works by friction.

GEL (aka JELLY)
Abbreviation for gelatin. 1) A DIFFUSER that softens the light of a STUDIO lamp. 2) A colored transparency used to change the color of a light source. For example, if a late afternoon look is desired at a LOCATION (or on a SET in a STUDIO), red-orange gels could be placed on the windows or in front of the lights to warm the color of the light.

GENERAL RELEASE
Instead of a limited engagement in a few theaters, a film is opened throughout the country in many theaters.

GENERATION
Each step involved in going from ORIGINAL NEGATIVE or tape, to final viewing (or listening) product. For example, to get from original 35mm negative to a RELEASE PRINT, you can (though not advisable) STRIKE a PRINT from the negative. That print would be second generation. More common is to go from a negative to a CRI to release print (third generation) or from negative to INTERPOSITIVE (IP) to DUPE NEGATIVE (Dupe Neg) - also considered three generations, as IP/dupe neg is considered to be one generation. The quality is as good as, if not better, than a print from a CRI. Generally the more generations away from the original, the poorer the quality of the final product. A 1/2 inch video cassette made from a 3/4 inch cassette will have poorer quality than a 1/2 inch cassette made from a print.

GENERATOR
A movable power source used on LOCATION (or as back-up power in a STUDIO) that runs on gasoline or diesel fuel.

GENERATOR OPERATOR
The person who turns on the GENERATOR at the beginning of the day and turns it off in the evening, and makes sure it stays in good running condition throughout PRODUCTION.

GENRE
A particular type of film *(e.g., comedy, WESTERN, sci-fi, mystery.)*

GIG
Slang for a job - usually used by actors and musicians.

GLASS SHOT
A technique used to create the illusion of expensive and difficult SETS and LOCATIONS without having to construct them or go there to shoot. The desired SCENE is painted on a part of a glass plate, then the action is shot through it, combining both on the film. *See also MATTE SHOT.*

GO
A go-ahead *(e.g., a "go" project.)*

GOBO *(aka FLAG)*
1) A black cloth, sheet, screen or mesh mounted on a stand to shield the camera from direct light during shooting, or to produce special lighting effects. 2) A sound absorbent, movable wall used in the STUDIO to minimize sound reverberation during recording.

GOFER *(aka RUNNER)*
A person who "goes for" this and that. *See PRODUCTION ASSISTANT.*

GOLDEN TIME *(aka GOLDEN HOURS)*
A form of overtime payment. If an employee is working in a STUDIO, or REPORTING TO a LOCATION within the STUDIO ZONE on a STRAIGHT TIME day, any time worked beyond 12 consecutive hours is calculated at double the hourly rate. If the employee, who does not fall under the ON CALL classification, works on a DOUBLE TIME day (Saturday, Sunday, holidays) in a

studio or on a location within the studio zone, any time beyond 12 consecutive hours is calculated at four times the basic hourly rate.

If the employee is working on a BUS TO location (where transportation is provided from the studio to the location) or DISTANT LOCATION on a straight time day, the hours are calculated at two and one-half times the basic hourly rate after fourteen consecutive hours have elapsed. On a double time day, the rate is five times the basic hourly rate after fourteen consecutive hours.

GOOSE (n.)
Slang for the camera and sound equipment truck.

GOOSE (v.)
To increase, push up *(e.g., "goose up" the sound.)*

GRADER
The LAB technician responsible for determining the density of a NEGATIVE. An experienced grader usually does this by eye.

GRADING
Determining and balancing the density of each FRAME of the NEGATIVE before printing so that the film is uniformly bright (or dark). This is done by a GRADER.

GRADUATED FILTER
A LENS attachment that allows different parts of the same SCENE to be photographed with different filter densities. For example, a SKY FILTER allows the sky to register more vividly without affecting the rest of the scene.

GREEN PRINT
A new positive print that has never been projected, or is not sufficiently dried for projection. Previously unprojected prints may need some lubrication to prevent them from jamming in the projector.

GREENSMAN
The CREW member responsible for DRESSING the SET with plants and trees, and maintaining them. Often, if a cut tree in a forest set (for example) has been on the set many days and has started to turn brown, the leaves or needles are simply painted green to make it look fresh and growing.

GREY CARD/GREY SCALE *(aka LILY)*
A standardized chart showing tonal gradations from white to grey to black. The card is photographed on the SET and then when the NEGATIVE is PROCESSED, the resulting IMAGE is compared by the LAB to the lab's grey card to check for correct tonal values. *See also COLOR BARS.*

GRIP
A general term for a crew member who provides the labor on the set in various departments - in the theatre they would be called stagehands. There are various grips for various departments: Lighting Grips, who trim, diffuse and mould lights; Construction Grips, who build sets, backdrops, etc; Dolly Grips, who lay and move DOLLY TRACKS, and push and pull the DOLLY, etc. *See also KEY GRIP, BEST BOY.*

GRIP, KEY
(see KEY GRIP).

GRIP PACKAGE
A typical grip package contains all the equipment required to adjust or manipulate lights and camera. It usually consists of: APPLE BOXES, packing quilts, SAND BAGS, gloves, SCRIMS, FLAGS, various light stands, mechanic and carpenter tools, a 12' by 12' frame (with the same size SILK and black cloth), a POLE CAT, box of wedges, HIGH ROLLERS and various REFLECTORS.

GRISWOLD
See MACHINE SPLICER.

GROSS
As reported in the TRADE PAPERS, generally the total BOX OFFICE receipts that a film has generated to date. However in most DISTRIBUTION, financing and participation agreements, the term is defined for purposes of specific agreement and means film RENTALS (monies received by the DISTRIBUTOR after the EXHIBITOR has retained his percentage) and license fees other than box office receipts.

GROSS DEAL
PROFIT participation in film rentals and not in NET PROFITS. These deals are usually reserved for the most powerful ACTORS, DIRECTORS or PRODUCERS.

GUARANTEE

1) A term usually used for ABOVE-THE-LINE personnel who have guarantees written into their contract *(i.e., a DIRECTOR with a contract stating that after the first PRINCIPAL PLAYER is hired, he/she is assured his/her entire salary whether or not the film is completed - or even shot.)* 2) A written legal agreement between two or more entities that an agreed-upon sum on money will be exchanged, either all at once or at pre-arranged intervals, when conditions specified in the contract have been met. These guarantees are used in PRE-SALES, DISTRIBUTION agreements, etc., and can help raise PRODUCTION FINANCING.

GUIDE TRACK

A SOUND TRACK recorded IN SYNC, that is used only as a guide to re-record the actual sound track under optimum conditions. It is not intended for use in the final film.

GYRO HEAD

A special CAMERA MOUNT with a flywheel to stabilize the camera when it PANS or TILTS.

H

HAIRDRESSER

A member of the CREW skilled and licensed to cut, color and style the hair of the actors on a production, and to use wigs, etc., when necessary. It is customary for a hairdresser to provide the necessary equipment (brushes, hair spray, etc.) and to be paid a weekly BOX RENTAL for it.

HAIR IN THE GATE
CAMERAMAN'S jargon for any foreign particle or matter in the camera gate.

HALATION
Any unwanted flare or halo that appears on the film. Usually caused by light reflected onto the EMULSION from the film BASE. To counteract this, most film manufacturers today put an ANTI-HALATION coating on the film that is then removed during PROCESSING.

HALF-APPLE
An APPLE BOX that is the same width and length as a normal apple, but only half as tall.

HALF LOAD
Term used in SPECIAL EFFECTS for one-half of a certain amount of explosive material used in guns and exploding devices.

HAND-CRANKED
The method by which motion pictures cameras were operated in the Silent Era. The CAMERAMAN had to approximate the 24 FRAME PER SECOND speed that produces normal motion. Motor driven cameras came into common use with the advent of sound when the camera speed had to be regulated and standardized in order to keep picture and sound IN SYNC. The concept of crank - ing has left its mark on modern terminology, however, because the terms OVERCRANK and UNDERCRANK are still used referring to SLOW MOTION and ACCELERATED MOTION CINEMA - TOGRAPHY.

HAND-HELD CAMERA
See CAMERA, HAND-HELD, STEADICAM.

HAND PROPS
Small items that are used by the actors in a SCENE *(e.g., a book, a gun, a newspaper)*. These items are bought, made or rented by the PROP DEPARTMENT.

HANDLER
See TRAINER, WRANGLER.

HAND SPLICER
See SPLICER.

HANGING MINIATURE
A MODEL of part of a SET that hangs 5-10 feet in front of the camera to give the illusion of something larger farther back in the set.

HAZE FILTER
A filter that reduces cloudy or foggy effects by absorbing blue and ultraviolet light. Haze is caused when light is scattered by dust and other particles.

HAZARD PAY
An additional payment made to an employee when working under conditions which are considered to be dangerous. For example, a helicopter CAMERA OPERATOR would be entitled to hazard pay.

HEAD
The beginning of a film or tape REEL. The opposite of TAIL.

HEADER
Cardboard strip about 4" wide and either 15" or 18 1/4" long on which are listed all the key elements that make up a SCRIPT BREAKDOWN. This strip is the guide for all the smaller PRODUCTION STRIPS comprised in a PRODUCTION STRIP BOARD.

HEAD SHOT
1) A CLOSE UP or shot that features the actor's head. 2) Slang for actors' resume photograph.

HEAD-ON SHOT
A shot that shows the action coming directly at the camera.

HEADS OUT *(or HEADS UP)*
Film wound so that it is ready for PROJECTION *(i.e., the first SCENES are on the outside of the roll.)* Film wound with the tail end out is called TAILS OUT or TAILS UP.

HELICOPTER MOUNT
See 'COPTER MOUNT, TYLER MOUNT.

HIATUS
A planned interruption in the PRODUCTION schedule. This almost always applies to episodic television when, after shooting all the shows for a season, the company shuts down for two or three months before resuming production.

HIGH ANGLE SHOT
A shot that looks down on the subject or action from high up.

HIGH FALL
A STUNT term indicating a jump or fall from an elevated place.

HIGH HAT/HI HAT (aka TOP HAT)
A small, low TRIPOD or CAMERA MOUNT used to shoot from very low ANGLES.

HIGH KEY LIGHTING
A lighting design used in color photography that produces an overall bright tone in a SCENE. Using high level illumination emphasizes the lighter tones of the GREY SCALE, resulting in a cheerier or brighter IMAGE.

HIGHLIGHT
To brighten or emphasize a specific object or area in a SCENE.

HIGHROLLER
A large, tall CENTURY STAND.

HIT
A huge success.

HIT YOUR MARKS
A slang expression meaning to move to the proper locations at the proper time according to how a scene has been blocked. Missing your marks can mean that the resulting scene will not be in proper focus.

HIT YOUR MARKS AND SAY YOUR LINES
A slang expression used by actors when they feel that the part they have been hired for does not require a great deal of creativity on their part.

HMI LIGHT
Abbreviation for Halogen Medium Iodide, a high-intensity ARC lamp that emits a very bright, daylight-BALANCED light. It uses alternating current, is lightweight and portable.

HOLD FRAME
An ANIMATION term that is the equivalent of live action OPTICAL FREEZE FRAME.

HONEYWAGON
A large, mobile unit with toilet facilities and dressing rooms for use by CAST and CREW.

HORSE
A stand to hold film REELS while feeding the film through the SYNCHRONIZER or VIEWER in the EDITING ROOM.

HOT SET
A set that has been fully DRESSED (including PROPS and RIGGING, etc.) and is ready for shooting, or is still being used for shooting.

HOT SPLICE *(aka CEMENT SPLICE)*
A method of permanently joining two pieces of film, usually reserved for ORIGINAL NEGATIVE or damaged RELEASE PRINTS. The splice is made by overlapping a very thin section of two pieces of film from which the EMULSION has been scraped. The BASE of one piece is dissolved into the base of the second, making a chemical weld. The two pieces of film become one. The alternate method is TAPE SPLICING in which a piece of mylar tape joins the two pieces of film. This is not permanent, and allows film being EDITED to be spliced and un-spliced as often as necessary. Since hot splicing requires the emulsion to be scraped off the areas being joined, at least one FRAME is lost. Tape splicing allows frame-for-frame splicing.

HOT SPLICER
A machine that controls the temperature of the cement (when making a HOT SPLICE) so it dries rapidly.

HOT SPOT
A portion of the IMAGE on the film that is BURNT OUT due to over lighting or insufficient GELLING of an area on the SET.

HOUSE NUT
A term used in EXHIBITION meaning *house expenses,* or how much it costs to operate a theater on a weekly basis. In a 90/10 agreement, the DISTRIBUTOR would retain 90% of the revenues received by the theater after the house expenses have been paid.

HYPHENATE
A person who has responsibility for more than one major function on a film. Woody Allen, Orson Welles, Charlie Chaplin, Buster Keaton, Barbra Streisand and Warren Beatty are some of the most famous hyphenates (WRITER/PRODUCER/DIRECTOR/ACTOR).

I

IATSE
Abbreviation for International Alliance of Theatrical and Stage Employees. The parent organization of some 1000 local UNIONS in North America representing every branch of PRODUCTION as well as employees in film DISTRIBUTION and EXHIBITION.

IDIOT CARDS
See CUE CARDS.

ILLUMINATION
Any natural or artificial light source that can cause an IMAGE to be recorded on film.

IMAGE
A photographic reproduction on film. The final choice of what will appear in the FRAME (hence be the image recorded on the film) while shooting is made by the DIRECTOR after consulting with the DIRECTOR OF PHOTOGRAPHY.

IMPROVISE
1) To create spontaneous ACTION or DIALOGUE. A departure from SCRIPTED material. 2) To devise immediate, alternate plans for PRODUCTION problems. *See WING IT.*

IN CAMERA
That part of the SCENE that is within the field of view of the camera at any particular moment while shooting.

INCANDESCENT LIGHT
Light produced by a glowing filament in the light bulb - warm glowing light as opposed to fluorescent light, which is cold and harsh. Not to be confused with a QUARTZ/HALOGEN light.

INCIDENT LIGHT
Light that falls directly on a subject as opposed to REFLECTED LIGHT. An incident light meter reads the amount of light actually falling on a subject as opposed to the amount of light reflected from that subject. *See EXPOSURE METER.*

INDEPENDENT CONTRACTOR
A person rendering services, but not as an employee on payroll. *See FREELANCE.*

INDEPENDENT PRODUCER
Formerly, the term meant a producer of low BUDGET and/or non-UNION films whose DISTRIBUTION would be limited - sometimes FOUR-WALLED. Now, the term can refer to any producer not under contract to a MAJOR STUDIO.

INDEPENDENT PRODUCTION
A production not financed by a MAJOR STUDIO. Nevertheless, a film produced independently may be DISTRIBUTED by a major.

INDIE PROD
Slang for INDEPENDENT PRODUCTION or INDEPENDENT PRODUCER.

INDIE PROD WITH A (FIVE) PIC PACK
TRADE PAPER slang meaning an INDEPENDENT PRODUCER with, in this case, a five-picture DEAL.

INFRARED
Invisible light rays whose wavelengths are longer (and slower) than those of visible light. If special FILTERS and infrared film STOCK are used, objects may be photographed in darkness.

INKIE
Slang for INCANDESCENT lamp used on the SET.

IN-PHASE
That situation in which two separate motors are running IN SYNC.

INSERT
A CLOSE UP detail of short duration, CUT into a SEQUENCE to explain some part of the ACTION or to assist CONTINUITY *(e.g., a hand circling an item in the want ads, a blood stain on the floor.)* *See SECOND UNIT.*

INSERT STAGE
A SOUND STAGE where inserts ar shot. There are firms that specialize in insert work for FEATURE FILMS and television production. Their facilities come fully equipped and staffed.

INSURANCE COVERAGE
As it is virtually impossible to predict accurately the cost of insurance on a FEATURE FILM due to so many variables, an average percentage figure of between two and four percent of the total NEGATIVE COST will be entered for insurance in the BUDGET. This estimate will depend on the SHOOTING SCHEDULE, LOCATIONS, CAST members, types of coverage needed *(e.g., NEGATIVE, DIRECTOR, errors and omissions, workmen's compensation, etc.)*

INSURANCE TAKE
See COVER SHOT.

IN SYNC
The situation in which the picture and its corresponding SOUND TRACK coincide and are running together at the proper speed. Any other situation is considered OUT OF SYNC. *See SYNCHRONIZATION.*

INT.
Abbreviation for INTERIOR.

INTERIOR
SHOTS which take place inside, and whose source of light is generally artificial. *See also EXTERIOR.*

INTEGRAL TRIPACK
A film with three layers of EMULSION, each sensitive to one of the PRIMARY COLORS, used to produce SEPARATION NEGA - TIVES in color photography.

INTENSIFICATION
A chemical process used to improve the quality of UNDER-EXPOSED NEGATIVES by increasing density and increasing the contrast of the IMAGE. *See THIN NEGATIVE.*

INTENSITY
The power of a light source as measured in CANDELAS or FOOTCANDLES.

INTERCUT
To alternate between different SEQUENCES of action while EDITING in order to make them appear to be happening concurrently. D.W.Griffith was the inventor of this technique. The most spectacular example of this in his work is the thrilling Ride of the Klan in *THE BIRTH OF A NATION.*

INTERLOCK
A system that allows separate picture and sound to be PROJECTED simultaneously IN SYNC. Usually used when screening WORK PRINT in various stages of EDITING.

INTERLOCK MOTOR
See MOTOR, SELSYN MOTOR.

INTERMITTENT MOVEMENT
The start/stop action that allows the film to advance at the speed of 24 FRAMES PER SECOND while stopping momentarily so that each FRAME can be EXPOSED or PROJECTED, on at a time.

INTERNEGATIVE/INTERNEG
(aka CRI - COLOR REVERSAL INTERNEGATIVE)
A negative made from the original negative, using REVERSAL FILM STOCK. This should not be confused with a DUPE NEGATIVE, which is a negative made from an INTERPOSITIVE.

INTEREST
A fee charged when money is borrowed, generally based on a percentage of the total sum at a specific lending rate.

INTERPOSITIVE *(Abbr. IP)*
A positive print made from the ORIGINAL NEGATIVE, used to make DUPE NEGATIVES, not used for PROJECTION. It can be recognized by its orange BASE. It is usually denser than positive RELEASE PRINTS. *See also CRI.*

IN THE CAN
1) A film that has completed PRINCIPAL PHOTOGRAPHY, or a SCENE that has been completed. 2) More specifically, EXPOSED film ready to be shipped to the LAB for PROCESSING.

INTROVISION
A relatively new, patented process for visual special effects that allows a matte shot to be seen while shooting the scene.

INVERSE SQUARE LAW
The efficiency of illumination (and sound) is inversely proportional to the square of the distance between the subject and its light source (or microphone). For example, if a subject receives ten CANDELAS of illumination when placed five feet away, it will only receive 2.5 candelas when placed ten feet away.

INVISIBLE SPLICE
The technique of A AND B ROLLING (NEGATIVE CUTTING) results in the splice between two pieces of film being invisible when printed.

IP
Abbreviation for INTERPOSITIVE.

IPS
Abbreviation for Inches Per Second. This is a unit of measurement indicating the speed at which sound is being recorded. Seven and one half IPS and higher are used for high fidelity music recording (30 IPS). Slower speeds are okay for recording speech.

IRIS *(aka DIAPHRAGM)*
The overlapping, adjustable pieces of metal or plastic which create the APERTURE in a LENS and controls the amount of light passing through that lens. A similar device exists on FOCUSING lamps to regulate the size of the area illuminated by the light. *See also CAMERA, F-STOP.*

J

JELLY
See GEL.

JENNY
Nickname for the GENERATOR used for power on LOCATION or for backup power in a STUDIO.

JUICER
Slang term for the CREW'S lamp operator - the person who installs and activates the lighting units on the SETS, and *"gives them the juice,"* so to speak.

JUMP CUT
A cut between SCENES or within a scene in which the action changes abruptly and unnaturally. A jump cut is achieved by taking out a section of film in the middle of a SHOT, or moving the camera closer or farther away without changing the ANGLE (or POV). Traditionally considered bad filmmaking, many filmmakers do this intentionally for effect *(e.g., Michaelangelo Antonioni's film BLOW-UP.)* This technique was brought into vogue by France's Nouvelle Vague (New Wave) directors, most specifically Jean-Luc Godard.

JUNIOR
A 1000-2000-watt LAMP. *See also SENIOR.*

KEG
A 750-watt SPOT that resembles a beer keg.

KEM
The trade name of a FLATBED EDITING machine. *See also STEENBECK, MOVIOLA.*

KEY GRIP
The head Grip of the department who works directly with the GAFFER and the DIRECTOR OF PHOTOGRAPHY. *See also GRIP, GRIP DEPARTMENT.*

KEY LIGHT
The main source of light in a scene that establishes the mood of the scene. The key light is usually the first light set by the DP, who then builds the rest of the lighting around it. *See LIGHTING.*

KEY NUMBER *(aka EDGE NUMBER)*
The manufacturer's serial numbers printed on the edge of the film, used by the NEGATIVE CUTTER when CONFORMING NEGATIVE to cut WORK PRINT. They are also used by the EDITOR when ordering EFFECTS - to tell the OPTICAL HOUSE where to begin and end the FADES and DISSOLVES. Edge numbers should not be confused with CODE NUMBERS.

KEY SECOND A.D.
On a PRODUCTION having more than one SECOND ASSISTANT DIRECTOR, the Key Second is in charge of the other Seconds, coordinating their tasks and reporting to the FIRST AD and to the PRODUCTION MANAGER. *See SECOND ASSISTANT DIRECTOR.*

KEYSTONE
Distorted shape of a PROJECTED IMAGE usually caused by tilting the PROJECTOR or the SCREEN. It can sometimes be caused by positioning the camera incorrectly.

KICKER *(aka SLICE LIGHT)*
A small light used for separating an object in the FOREGROUND form the BACKGROUND - outlining faces or hair, etc.

KILL
To turn off *(e.g., "kill the baby" means, turn off the small spotlight.)*

KINESCOPE
The recording of live television off of a TV screen onto film. It is usually of poor quality, although it was the only way to record television before videotape.

KIT RENTAL
See BOX RENTAL.

KLEIG LIGHTS
Powerful, open-ARC floodlights used in front of theaters for gala openings, also used in PRODUCTION for effect.

KOOK *(aka Cookie, Cucaloris, Kukaloris)*
A metal, wooden or plastic screen with variously shaped cut-out areas that, when placed in front of a light source, casts a variety of shadows on an otherwise monotonous surface.

L

LABORATORY *(Abbr. LAB)*
The place where EXPOSED film is DEVELOPED, PROCESSED and printed.

LACQUERING
A protective coating on film that prevents abrasions to the surface.

LAP DISSOLVE
See DISSOLVE, A AND B CUTTING.

LATENSIFICATION
Means of increasing the density of the LATENT IMAGE by EXPOSING the undeveloped NEGATIVE to extremely low light for a long period of time. This process increases shadow detail in cases of extreme UNDEREXPOSURE.

LATENT IMAGE
The image present chemically on EXPOSED, unprocessed film. Once DEVELOPED, it becomes a TRUE IMAGE.

LATERAL FLICKER
An effect caused by PANNING too quickly.

LATITUDE
The range in which film can be OVEREXPOSED or UNDEREXPOSED and still provide a satisfactory IMAGE. The faster the speed of the film (the higher the ASA), the greater the flexibility in choosing F-STOPS.

LAUGH TRACK *(aka CANNED LAUGHTER)*
A tape recording of various kinds of laughter that is used on television shows when there is no live audience, or when more laughter is needed. The laugh track can be modulated and controlled by a laugh track technician.

LAVENDER
Slang for FINE GRAIN MASTER POSITIVE used in making black and white PRINTS, so called because of the former color of its BASE.

LAY IN
EDITING terminology meaning CUT in, or put in, as in *lay in* EFFECTS, *lay in* the sound, etc.

LAYOUT
A detailed plan of all ACTION, movement, SPECIAL EFFECTS, lights, etc. prepared prior to SHOOTING *(e.g., to lay out a SCENE)*.

LEAD
PRINCIPAL PLAYER (actor or actress).

LEADER
A length of blank or black film used to connect SHOTS in the WORK PRINT, or attached to the HEAD and TAIL of each REEL in RELEASE PRINTS to allow the reel to be threaded into the machine and run off of it without interfering with the picture. *See also ACADEMY LEADER, UNIVERSAL LEADER, FILM LEADER.*

LEAD MAN
The person responsible to the SET DECORATOR and head of the SWING GANG in the SET DRESSING department.

LEAK LIGHT
Unwanted light that can be eliminated by using a GOBO, BARN-DOORS or a MASK.

LEGS
1) When a picture in RELEASE has enough drawing power to keep the audiences walking into the theaters each week, it is said to have *legs*.
2) Slang for TRIPOD.

LENS
An optical device that focuses the IMAGE onto the film. There are three basic type of lenses (divided according to FOCAL LENGTH): Normal, covering a medium field; WIDE ANGLE, covering an extensive field of view, but causing a reduction in the proportional size of IMAGES; and TELEPHOTO, covering a limited field, but having magnifying properties. A ZOOM LENS combines all three capabilities, although with a slight reduction in quality. PRIME LENSES have a single capability and give best quality.

LENS ABERRATION
See ABERRATION, LENS.

LENS ADAPTER
A device that is attached to the front of the camera to handle other than normal lenses *(e.g., 2X extender)*.

LENS BARREL
The cylindrical tube that protects the ELEMENTS, or parts of the lens apparatus.

LENS COVER *(aka LENS CAP)*
Plastic or metal cover that protects the lens when not in use.

LENS COATING
See ANTI-HALATION.

LENS HOOD
A shield that prevents unwanted light from striking the lens surface.

LENS SPEED
The ability of a lens to admit light. The greater the size of the APERTURE (and, conversely, the smaller the number of the F-STOP), the faster the lens. A fast lens can capture IMAGES in low light conditions.

LENS TURRET
A disc in front of the camera upon which are mounted several (usually four) lenses. Any of the lenses can be brought into position and locked into place by rotating the turret. These are not used very much any more.

LEVEL
1) Position of the camera when it is perfectly parallel to the horizontal plane. 2) In sound recording, the decibel range for the best sound reproduction. 3) Sound volume.

LIBRARY *(FILM/MUSIC)*
1) A place where films and STOCK FOOTAGE are stored for viewing. Most film libraries are temperature controlled and have some EDITING capabilities. 2) A place where a collection of pre-recorded music is kept and listening facilities are available.

LIBRARY SHOT *(aka STOCK FOOTAGE)*
Previously existing SCENES or SHOTS taken from a collection that would be too expensive, too difficult or impossible to shoot over again *(e.g., aerial views of New York, ships sinking, battle scenes, cars on the highway, street scenes from the 1940's, theater or nightclub marquees.)*

LIGHT, ARTIFICIAL
Light that has been created and does not come from natural sources such as the sun or the moon.

LIGHT BOX
A box with a translucent top and a light inside used for viewing film or transparencies or film that is being CUT. Also used in ANIMATION.

LIGHT, HARD
Bright light that produces high contrast and harsh shadows. It is usually less flattering to actors and is used to create certain effects. The opposite is soft or DIFFUSED light.

LIGHTING
The illumination of a SCENE to achieve a desired mood or atmosphere in a photographic IMAGE. Lighting is the responsiblity of the DIRECTOR OF PHOTOGRAPHY, in consultation with the DIRECTOR. Because lights are the most cumbersome of film equipment, setting the lighting can be difficult and very time consuming. There are four types of lighting that can be used: KEY LIGHTS, FILL

LIGHTS, BACK LIGHTS and KICK LIGHTS. Key lights are the main source of lighting on the SET, used to provide the principal illumination of the scene. Fill lights are used to compliment and supplement the key lights, to lighten shadows or reduce contrast. Backlighting is used to illuminate the BACKGROUND and add depth to the image. KICKERS (kick lights) outline hair and face, and accent details.

LIGHTING CAMERAMAN
British term for DIRECTOR OF PHOTOGRAPHY.

LIGHT METER
See EXPOSURE METER.

LILY
A set of COLOR BARS and/or GREY SCALE shot at the beginning or end of a roll to assist the LAB in checking color accuracy and tonal values.

LIMBO SET
A set in which a minimal amount of BACKGROUND, PROPS or other devices that would establish a specific location are used, excluding all but the principal action or subject.

LIMITED RELEASE
A film that is shown in a small, specific area for the purpose of gauging audience reaction, or finding an audience. This is called test marketing. If a film is known to have limited appeal, or a limited audience (most foreign films, art films, etc.), or limited resources, it goes into limited release to limit the risk of financial loss.

LINE PRODUCER
The supervisor of both ABOVE-THE-LINE and BELOW-THE-LINE elements during PRODUCTION. The PRODUCTION MANAGER reports to the line producer on below-the-line matters.

LINING UP
1) Positioning the camera and actors and adjusting the lights before making a SHOT. 2) For OPTICAL EFFECTS, lining up means SYNCHING the IP to the WORK PRINT.

LIP SYNC
1) Technique wherein an actor moves his or her lips in synchronization with a pre-recorded song to create the illusion that he/she is singing. 2) The technique for re-recording DIALOGUE in a picture. The actor

says his or her lines while the picture is run, trying to sync the words with the picture on the screen. *See ADR, LOOPING, DUBBING.*

LIQUID GATE *(aka WET GATE, SUBMERGED PRINTING)*
A procedure for minimizing abrasions and scratches on film while it is being PRINTED. This is done by an OPTICAL HOUSE.

LIVE ACTION
Real actors filmed on SETS or at real LOCATIONS as opposed to ANIMATION or SPECIAL EFFECTS made to look like real action.

LIVE SOUND *(aka LIVE RECORDING)*
Dialogue and BACKGROUND sound recorded during PRINCIPAL PHOTOGRAPHY and not created later in a sound studio.

LIVING ALLOWANCE *(aka PER DIEM)*
On overnight LOCATION shooting, this is a fixed amount of money that is paid in lieu of the PRODUCTION COMPANY'S direct payment of an employee's expenses while living away from home.

LOAD
To put film in the camera (or MAGAZINE) before shooting.

LOADER
When several cameras are used, this Camera Department crew member assists the SECOND ASSISTANT CAMERAMAN and loads film into the magazines.

LOADING ROOM
A small DARKROOM on a SET or in a vehicle used for loading and unloading MAGAZINES.

LOCAL LOCATION
Any spot within a thirty mile radius of the UNION agreed-upon center, to be used for shooting a film or television show, or any shooting location where cast and crew does not have to spend the night. In Los Angeles, it is usually thirty miles from the intersection of La Cienega and Beverly Boulevard. In Manhattan, a local location is defined as any place between 125th Street and the Battery (the southern tip of Manhattan.) *See also STUDIO ZONE.*

LOCATION
Any locale used for shooting away from the STUDIO. Location shooting provides special problems for PRODUCTION MANAGERS who must arrange for food, shelter, toilet facilities, transportation to

and from for CAST and CREW plus GENERATORS and other special equipment. LOCAL LOCATIONS are near a studio. Cast and crew will usually have a Report To Location CALL for a certain time, then return home that night. Distant, or Overnight Locations are any locations farther than local locations where cast and crew are obliged to stay overnight, and usually work a six day a week schedule.

LOCATION ACCOUNTANT
(aka PRODUCTION ACCOUNTANT, LOCATION AUDITOR)
The person assigned to account for all the money spent while shooting a picture on location.

LOCATION AUDITOR
See LOCATION ACCOUNTANT.

LOCATION FEE
The compensation paid for the use of a site and facilities when shooting a motion picture or television show.

LOCATION MANAGER
The person who reads the SCRIPT to find out what locations are needed, SCOUTS for locations, evaluates their suitability then takes photographs which are shown to the DIRECTOR and PRODUCTION DESIGNER. After a location has been approved, the location manager arranges for permission and negotiates the terms for using the location for shooting. He/she is then responsible for organizing all the details that relate to that location - permits, parking, catering, police, firemen, etc. The location manager is responsible for drawing up a BUDGET for all locations.

LONG FOCUS LENS *(aka TELEPHOTO LENS)*
A lens with a FOCAL LENGTH longer than that of a normal lens. Its main ability is to photograph distant subjects as if they were close up. When a telephoto is used, the DEPTH OF FIELD is decreased *(i.e., the BACKGROUND is flattened or obscured.)*

LONG SHOT *(Abbr. LS)*
A wide shot of the principal subject. The camera is positioned far enough away to be able to identify the subject in its setting, but not see any great amount of detail. Long shots are used mainly for ESTABLISHING and MASTER SHOTS.

LOOP (n.)
1) The length of film in the camera or projector not engaged in the SPROCKETS, that absorbs the vibrations of the projector or camera

motor as the film passes through (momentarily stops at) the GATE. 2) A length of magnetic sound film or tape joined head to tail, that forms a circle, or loop, so that the recording is repeated again and again as it goes over the player head.

LOOP (v.)
The act of DUBBING in (LOOPING), or replacing, newly recorded sounds or speech with previously recorded sounds or speech. Usually the principal actors will be called back during POST PRODUCTION to re-record lines that were not recorded properly, or need to be changed or added. *See also ADR.*

LOSE
Get rid of as in, *"Let's lose that extra lamp on the set."* See *EIGHTY SIX.*

LOT
The area on which a STUDIO is located (office buildings, SOUND STAGES, dressing rooms, etc.) with guards at the front gate to regulate entry of non-employees. *See STUDIO (LOT).*

LOW-ANGLE SHOT
A shot taken with the camera close to the ground, looking up at the subject.

LOW KEY
A SCENE that is lit at the lower end of the GREY SCALE, using dim illumination to produce lots of shadows.

LS
Abbreviation for LONG SHOT.

LUMINAIRE
A self-contained light, complete with lamp, housing and its own stand.

M

MACHINE SPLICER
A splicer operated with the hands and feet, used for cutting the NEGATIVE. The most common brand name is GRISWOLD. *See SPLICER.*

MAGAZINE
A film container or cassette that fits on the camera with two light-proof compartments, one for the unexposed film, and one for the film that has already been exposed. Most magazines can hold up to 2,000 feet of film, and make it easy to load film into the camera (by changing magazines) in broad daylight. The magazine itself must be loaded in a DARKROOM or CHANGING BAG.

MAGIC HOUR
Twilight. The time between sundown and darkness when the light is very warm, the sky is a magical deep blue, and shadows are long. An example of SCENES shot at Magic Hour is Terrence Malick's film, DAYS OF HEAVEN.

MAGNETIC FILM (MAG FILM)
A perforated film BASE the same size as motion picture film, coated with iron oxide instead of light-sensitive EMULSION, for recording sound. This is used for EDITING, not PRODUCTION sound. The PERFORATIONS allow SYNCHRONIZATION with the picture track.

MAGNETIC RECORDING
Sound recorded IN SYNC with motion picture film on magnetic tape that will be transferred later to MAG FILM for EDITING, then, after the final MIX is completed, transferred back to film on an OPTICAL TRACK.

MAGNETIC STRIPE
A coating of ferromagnetic iron oxide that runs along the edge of per - forated 70mm DOLBY film onto which sound is recorded.

MAGNETIC TAPE
A high quality polyester or MYLAR based tape coated with a substance containing iron oxide, for recording sound, or for recording sound and picture on videotape. Professional size is 1/4 inch and generally runs between 7 1/2 and 15 IPS for high quality recording. This is five times faster than home recording.

MAG/OPTICAL PRINT
A RELEASE PRINT containing both magnetic and optical SOUND TRACKS for use in theaters that have either system:

MAIN TITLE (S)
Although specifically referring to the TITLE CARD containing the name of the film, it more generally refers to all CREDITS appearing at the beginning of the film. Under the terms of the DGA contract, the DIRECTOR'S credit is the last to appear before the beginning of the film.

MAKE-UP
Creams, powders, mascara, eye liner, etc., applied to the faces, and sometimes the bodies, of the ACTORS and EXTRAS in a film. Make-up can enhance the features of the actor, create an effect *(e.g., old age)* or illusion, cover a blemish or scar (or create a blemish or scar or wound) or transform the actor into a different person altogether *(e.g., PLANET OF THE APES)*. Sometimes elaborate make-up will require many hours to apply *(e.g., Dustin Hoffman in LITTLE BIG MAN, the actors in PLANET OF THE APES, David Naughton in AMERICAN WEREWOLF IN LONDON)* resulting in an exceptionally early MAKE-UP CALL.

MAKE-UP ARTIST
A member of the PRODUCTION CREW skilled (and usually licensed) in applying make-up on the actors - but only from the top of the head to the breast bone, and from the elbow to the fingertips. A Body Make-

Up Artist applies make-up to any other parts of the actor's body. *See also SPECIAL EFFECTS.*

MAKE UP CALL

The time when the actor must report to the SET to have his or her make-up applied in order to be ready to shoot a SCENE. The time required can be anywhere from 15 minutes to 7 hours each day, as was the case for Lou Gosset Jr. in *ENEMY MINE*. The make-up call is determined by counting backwards from the time the actor will be needed on the set (the CALL time). For example, an 8:30 AM call would have meant a 1:30 or 2:30 AM make-up call for poor Lou Gosset.

MARKS

Small pieces of masking tape (or chalk marks) put on the floor to identify certain positions: where the camera should stop DOLLYING, where the actor should stop his/her motion so that the scene being shot will be in proper focus, etc. In a scene where many actors are moving around, each actor will be assigned a different color tape (chalk) so as not to get confused. Before the scene is shot, the marks are removed so that they will not accidentally show up on the screen.

MARRIED PRINT

British term for COMPOSITE PRINT.

MASK

1) A black frame that outlines the SCREEN in a movie theater that can be altered for different ASPECT RATIO formats. 2) A device that covers part of the FRAME in black *(i.e., to create the effect of looking through a telescope or a pair of binoculars.)* This is done OPTICALLY after the film has been shot and processed rather in front of the LENS. 3) A FLAG or GOBO used to keep unwanted light off the camera lens.

MASTER *(aka MASTER POSITIVE)*

Film or tape from which DUPE NEGATIVES are made for STRIKING RELEASE PRINTS - or, in the case of sound or video tape, the material from which subsequent listening or viewing copies are made. *See CRI, IP.*

MASTER SCENE

A primary DIALOGUE or ACTION scene in which characters are developed, plot is advanced, etc.

MASTER SHOT
An uninterrupted, complete shot of an entire scene, and to which all other shots in the scene are related. For example, in a scene where two actors are talking, the uninterrupted shooting of the entire scene with all DIALOGUE is the Master, which is usually completed to satisfaction before going in for COVERAGE (CLOSE UPS, OVER-THE-SHOULDER shots, etc.) The Master shot itself can be used without coverage, if shot with that intent.

MATCH
1) To repeat the ACTION and/or DIALOGUE exactly so that the CONTINUITY of the subsequent shots is maintained so they can be cut into the MASTER SHOT. 2) To line up the FINAL CUT WORK PRINT with the NEGATIVE so they CONFORM FRAME by frame, in order to cut the negative so RELEASE PRINTS can be made.

MATRICES
A set of three pieces of film used to make color PRINTS by the three STRIP TECHNICOLOR process. Each strip is sensitive to one of the PRIMARY COLORS (red, green and blue) and each contains part of the final IMAGE. Each matrix absorbs a dye and transfers the color to the required area of the FRAME as it comes into contact with the RELEASE PRINT STOCK.

MATTE
A specially designed mask with one or more specified areas cut out so that when placed on a camera or PRINTER LENS, the areas not masked are EXPOSED. Mattes are used in SPECIAL EFFECTS for combining separate IMAGES onto one piece of film, changing BACKGROUNDS or the tone of an image. *See MATTE BOX, MATTE SHOT, SPECIAL EFFECTS.*

MATTE ARTIST
A member of the SPECIAL EFFECTS department who designs and helps construct BACKGROUNDS or MATTES for MATTE SHOTS. One of the legendary matte artists is Albert Whitlock, whose work appears in such films as *THE BIRDS, MARNIE, THE STING, EARTHQUAKE, SHIP OF FOOLS.* He won an ACADEMY AWARD for his work on *THE HINDENBURG.*

MATTE BOX *(aka SPECIAL EFFECTS BOX)*
An adjustable FILTER holder attached to the front of the LENS. It shields the lens from unwanted light, and holds mattes and filters in place when shooting. *See MATTE SHOT.*

MATTE SCREEN
A specially treated projection screen, in which the brightness of the images appears the same from all viewing angles.

MATTE SHOT
A shot combining many layers of moving elements in a live action SCENE with a pro-photographed BACKGROUND. *See also TRAVELING MATTE.*

MCU
Abbreviation for MEDIUM CLOSE UP.

MEAL PENALTY
A fine paid to a crew or cast member who has not been given enough time off for a meal, or the beginning of whose meal break has been delayed longer than permitted by union regulations.

MEAT AXE
Slang for a rod usually used on scaffolding to hold SCRIMS or FLAGS.

MEDIUM CLOSE UP *(Abbr. MCU)*
A shot in between a CLOSE and MEDIUM SHOT.

MEDIUM LONG SHOT *(Abbr. MLS)*
A shot in between a MEDIUM and LONG SHOT, with the subject in the middle distance, not in the foreground or background.

MERCURY VAPOR LAMP
A small ARC which emits a bluish light and is used mainly for close-up work. The arcs are vaporized mercury sealed in glass vacuum tubes.

M&E TRACK
Abbreviation for Music and Effects Track. The SOUND TRACK containing everything but the DIALOGUE. It is particularly useful when doing foreign language versions, as new dialogue can be recorded without interfering with the music or effects.

METTEUR-EN-SCENE
The French term for DIRECTOR which came from the stage, meaning, literally, the person who places (the action) in the scene. The more modern term is REALISATEUR.

MICRO-CINEMATOGRAPHY
Photographing objects too small for ordinary LENSES, using a combination of a microscope and a motion picture camera.

MICROPHONE BOOM *(aka BOOM)*
An adjustable arm that moves the mike into position above the range of view of the camera when shooting. It is handled by the BOOM OPERATOR.

MIDGET
A small FILL LIGHT SPOT that uses 50-200-watt lamps.

MILEAGE MONEY
Money paid to CAST and CREW members during PRODUCTION when they drive their own vehicles to a LOCATION.Compensation is a specified amount, set by UNION contract. It is presently $.30 per mile.

MINIATURE
A tiny scale model of a SET used for shooting SPECIAL EFFECTS. Often used when a SCENE is too expensive or difficult to build life-size. Miniature art work has become a highly specialized branch of the special effects department, due to the special equipment required and the complexity of the work. *See also MODEL.*

MINIBRUTE
A 650-watt light used for supplementing sunlight on outdoor LOCATIONS and for FILL LIGHT for color work in the STUDIO.

MINILIGHT
A compact light with a REFLECTOR and BARN DOORS, used mostly for FILL LIGHT.

MINIMOUNT
A stable CAMERA MOUNT that can be attached to planes, heli - copters, cars or boats.

MINIMUM CALL
The fewest number of hours for which an actor or CREW member is entitled to be paid regardless of whether or not the hours are worked.

MIRROR SHUTTER
A camera shutter with reflecting mirrors that allows the CAMERA OPERATOR to view the same IMAGE he is shooting without having to compensate for PARALLAX. *See also VIEWFINDER.*

MISE-EN-SCENE
French term for direction. The direct translation is "to put into the scene" (stage). *See also METTEUR-EN-SCENE.*

MITCHELL
A motion picture camera usually used in STUDIOS and not for LOCATION work due to its size and lack of portability.

MIX
Combining separate SOUND TRACKS into a single sound track on a single piece of MAGNETIC TAPE with three to four separate channels. It is then TRANSFERRED onto an OPTICAL TRACK (or MAG/- OPTICAL TRACK) for use in the COMPOSITE PRINT. The mix, or re-recording, is done on a MIXING CONSOLE by the MIXER (in a film's CREDITS listed as RE-RECORDING MIXER). *See also DUBBING.*

MIXER, PRODUCTION *(aka SOUND RECORDIST)*
Chief sound engineer on the SET whose primary responsibility is to achieve the best recorded sound possible during PRODUCTION.

MIXER, RE-RECORDING
The chief sound engineer responsible for the final MIX when all of the different SOUND TRACKS, including DIALOGUE, MUSIC and all EFFECTS TRACKS are put together and balanced to make the picture's final sound track.

MLS
Abbreviation for MEDIUM LONG SHOT.

MOO PRINT
A LABORATORY term for a perfect print.

MOCK-UP
A full-scale MODEL of an object, built on the SET to simulate the real thing *(e.g., the plane in AIRPORT.)*

MODEL
A scale duplicate of a real object, used when it would be too difficult or oo costly to shoot the real thing. *See also MINIATURE, MOCK-UP.*

MODELING LIGHT
Light which emphasizes the contour and texture of a subject. Also called the Contour Key, it is aimed at the subject in the opposite direction of the KEY LIGHT. *See also LIGHTING.*

MODULATION
Variations in the amplitude, phase or frequency of continuous sound waves, usually in recorded sound.

MONITOR
A video screen, used with a video camera during filming or taping to check the accuracy of EXPOSURE, or the quality of an IMAGE or sound, or to check the quality of a performance as seen by the camera.

MONOCHROMATIC
A term usually applied to black and white photography, but also meaning an IMAGE that is composed of a single color, or tonal gradations of a single color.

MONOPACK
A color film in which there are three separate layers of EMULSION, each sensitive to one of the PRIMARY COLORS. *See also INTEGRAL TRIPACK.*

MONOPOLE
An adjustable device for hanging STUDIO lights.

MONTAGE
1) A series of SHOTS (usually not continuous) that CUT and/or DISSOLVE into one another to tell a story within the story, or denote the passage of time, often without DIALOGUE. 2) French term for EDITING.

MORTARS
Steel containers used by the SPECIAL EFFECTS team when creating explosions during shooting.

MOS *(aka WILD PICTURE)*
Abbreviation for Mit Out (without) Sound, literally, a SHOT made without accompanying, SYNCHRONIZED sound. When such a shot is made, MOS is written on the SLATE along with the other usual information. It came into use in the early days of sound films when a large number of sound technicians happened to be German. Legend has it that DIRECTOR Lothar Mendes (a German himself) was the person

who coined the term when he instructed the CREW to do the next shot "mit out sound". The term stuck and is used to this day.

MOTOR
A mechanized device that causes motion. Most professional motion picture cameras are driven by electrical motors which provide a constant speed of operation so that the sound can be recorded IN SYNC. VARIABLE SPEED MOTORS, which can be noisier, are used for shooting SLOW or ACCELERATED MOTION (shot MOS) and can be regulated from 4 FPS to 50 FPS.

MOW
Abbreviation for Movie of the Week.

MOVIOLA
The trademark of a device used for viewing INTERLOCKED picture and sound tracks. It is used extensively in EDITING for building SOUND TRACKS. It has variable speeds and can be stopped at a single FRAME so that the EDITOR can mark the CUTS, OPTICAL EFFECTS, etc. The film runs up and down through the viewer instead of side to side like a FLATBED.

MOVEMENT LIST
An information sheet listing the means by which everyone connected with the PRODUCTION is getting to and from a LOCATION.

MPAA
Abbreviation for Motion Picture Association of America, the organi - zation that gives films and their advertising (TRAILERS, etc.) their RATINGS. All major DISTRI-BUTORS are members. The MPAA also employs ex-FBI agents to track down film pirates both in the United States and abroad. They are also the chief lobbying arm of the film industry. They represent the interests of major distributors of the motion picture industry in financial, legal, ethical, trade and foreign trade matters. The Motion Picture Export Assn. (MPEA) is the foreign office of the MPAA, and acts as a trade organization for the American motion picture industry abroad.

MPAA CODE SEAL
A certification that a film, its TRAILERS and advertising have been made and rated in conformity with the regulations and standards of the MPAA.

MS
Abbreviation for MEDIUM SHOT.

MULTI-BEAM
A small quartz iodine light used for indoor and outdoor LIGHTING.

MULTIBROAD
A light that can be focused by turning a knob.

MULTICAMERA
The use of two or more cameras to shoot a SCENE from different ANGLES simultaneously. Recommended for large ACTION SHOTS or shots that are difficult (expensive) to create *(e.g., a car driving over a cliff, a bridge exploding)*.

MULTI-DUTY MOTOR
A special motor that can drive camera and sound equipment IN SYNC. *See also CRYSTAL MOTOR.*

MULTI-HEAD PRINTER
A printer that can make more than one copy of a film at a time.

MULTI-LAYER FILM
See MONO PACK, INTEGRAL TRI-PACK.

MULTIPLE-IMAGE SHOT
A shot in which the same image appears repeated in a FRAME. This EFFECT can either be achieved OPTICALLY or with a special, multi-image LENS.

MULTI-SCREEN
A PROJECTION system using several INTERLOCKED projectors and large abutting screens. *See CINERAMA.*

MURAL
A large painting or photograph used as a BACKGROUND, both indoors and out.

"MURDER YOUR WIFE" BRICK
Imitation brick first used during and so-named after the film starring Jack Lemmon.

MUSIC BRIDGE
A musical segment that provides the transition between SCENES and/or moods. *See also SEGUE.*

MUSIC CONTRACTOR
The person responsible for hiring musicians and coordinating all business and financial activities for music (recording) sessions. He/she must be present at all recording sessions.

MUSIC CUE SHEET
A list by REEL of all music cues with each COMPOSER and publisher, to be used for royalties and licensing.

MUSIC, FILM
See SCORE.

MUSIC LIBRARY
See LIBRARY.

MUSIC MIXER
The sound person responsible for controlling, balancing and mixing the film's musical SCORE. He/she is part of a team of re-recording MIXERS who prepare the final SOUND TRACK.

MUSIC TRACK
That channel of the SOUNDTRACK onto which the music is recorded, separate and distinct from the DIALOGUE and the EFFECTS TRACKS.

MUTE
British term for a PRINT or NEGATIVE with no SOUND TRACK.

MYLAR
An extremely strong plastic material onto which the ferromagnetic coating is applied for video and audio tape.

N

NABET
Abbreviation for NATIONAL ALLIANCE OF BROADCAST ENGINEERS AND TECHNICIANS.

NAGRA
The most widely used brand of self-contained CRYSTAL SYNC sound recorder used for recording sound on the SET or on LOCATION. The Nagra was responsible for freeing filmmakers from the STUDIO because it enabled them to produce studio-quality sound with a small, very portable machine. Stefan Kudelski received an ACADEMY AWARD for developing and perfecting the Nagra.

NARRATION
VOICE OVER (VO) commentary that advances the story line.

NARRATIVE
The story line.

NARROW GAUGE FILM
Most common: 16mm. The quality is not as good as 35 mm, but it is less expensive. It is often used for DOCUMENTARY, industrial and student films, and also for commercial and research applications.

NATIONAL ALLIANCE OF BROADCAST ENGINEERS AND TECHNICIANS

A national labor organization affiliated with the AFL-CIO, formed originally for radio technicians and engineers, and later expanded to include television technicians and engineers. When television executives decided to do their own film projects*(i.e., television films, MOVIES OF THE WEEK, MINISERIES)*, an agreement was worked out with IATSE (the union for film stagehands and technicians). Now NABET is generally used for television PRODUCTION and IATSE for film production, though these days (especially in New York) NABET crews are often used on low BUDGET FEATURE FILMS.

NATURAL LIGHT

Any light that is non-artificial *(e.g., sunlight, moonlight.)*

ND

1) Abbreviation for Non-Descript *(e.g., this SCENE will require 25 ND office worker EXTRAS.)* 2) Abbreviation for Neutral Density *(i.e., a NEUTRAL DENSITY FILTER or GEL that evenly reduces the amount of light on the film or on the SCENE being lit on the SET.)*

NEGATIVE

EXPOSED and PROCESSED film whose IMAGE is the opposite of the original subject *(i.e., the reverse of a POSITIVE.)* The term sometimes refers to unexposed film STOCK *(aka RAW STOCK)*, or stock in the camera before processing.

NEGATIVE COST

All expenses required to achieve the final NEGATIVE, from which RELEASE PRINTS are made. The term, or an equivalent term, is usually defined in financing and participation agreements. These special definitions vary from contract to contract, especially with respect to indirect costs *(e.g., OVERHEAD)* and CONTINGENCY costs, and will govern the interpretation of each respective contract.

NEGATIVE CUTTER

The person who CONFORMS the NEGATIVE, FRAME by frame, to the cut WORK PRINT.

NEGATIVE CUTTING

The process of matching or CONFORMING the negative FRAME by frame to the EDITED WORK PRINT, in order to produce the different GENERATIONS that lead to the ANSWER PRINT, then RELEASE PRINTS. The negative cutter uses the KEY NUMBERS to guide him or her.

NEGATIVE PICK-UP
A term used to describe an agreement between a DISTRIBUTOR and the PRODUCER of a motion picture whereby the distribution company agrees to pay a certain amount of money for the rights to distribute the film. The money is usually not released to the producer until the film is finished - delivery of the completed and cut NEGATIVE. This is the opposite of PRE-PRODUCTION financing. If the pick-up deal is with a MAJOR STUDIO, the producer can usually take that agreement to a bank where it can be discounted *(i.e., converted into money for a fee)*. Many productions are financed, or partially financed this way.

NET PROFITS
See PROFITS.

NETWORK
A major television company, responsible for the creation and development of programming, its transmission to the interconnected stations comprising the network's affiliates *(i.e., network owned and operated stations plus non-network owned and operated stations)* along with the development of technological advancements and the sale of air time and programming to advertisers (sponsors). The major networks in the United States are ABC, CBS, NBC and PBS.

NEUTRAL DENSITY FILTER
A filter for the camera LENS that reduces EXPOSURE and contrast without changing the color. *See also ND.*

NEWTON RINGS
Colored, odd-shaped circles that appear on film as a result of light bouncing between two smooth surfaces *(e.g., FILTERS on a LENS) while shooting.*

NG
Abbreviation for No Good. This is usually used in reference to a bad TAKE.

NIGHT EFFECT
See DAY-FOR-NIGHT.

NIGHT-FOR-NIGHT
Night SEQUENCES that are actually shot at night. For the most part, night exteriors, or night interiors where night exteriors need to be seen *(i.e., through windows)*, are shot night-for-night. *See also DAY-FOR-NIGHT.*

NIGHT PREMIUM
An adjustment made to the basic rate of pay per various UNIONS and GUILDS, for work conducted after a certain hour, usually 8:00 PM.

NITRATE BASE
Obsolete, highly flammable film BASE used in early days of filmmaking. *See also ACETATE BASE, SAFETY BASE.*

NOISE
Any unwanted or distracting sounds picked up during recording.

NON-THEATRICAL
The film market designated for limited DISTRIBUTION among specialized audiences, not in theaters. The non-theatrical market includes television, CABLE, schools, libraries, film clubs, inflight airlines, the Armed Forces, etc. The largest, and newest non-theatrical market today is video cassettes.

NOTCH
A mark on the film's edge that shows where an adjustment in printing density is to be made. These days this is done by computer.

NUMBERING MACHINE *(aka ENCODING MACHINE)*
A device used by ASSISTANT EDITORS to print CODE NUMBERS at regular intervals on the edge of the WORK PRINT.

O

OC
Abbreviation for OFF CAMERA

OFF CAMERA *(Abbr. OC, aka OFF- SCREEN)*
Not seen by the camera.

OFF MIKE
Out of the primary range of the microphone.

OFF-REGISTER
Accidental or deliberate rocking effect resulting from camera vibration. Explosions are sometimes made to appear more real by intentionally doing this.

OFF-SCREEN *(Abbr. OS)*
Refers to a sound or action that comes from, or happens in an area OFF-CAMERA, so it is not seen on the screen when the film is PROJECTED.

OLD-TIMER
Slang term for a flexible pole that holds FLAGS or SCRIMS.

OMNIDIRECTIONAL MICROPHONE
(Abbr. OMNIMIKE)
A microphone that is receptive to sounds coming from all directions.

ON A BELL
When a film company is actually shooting, a bell is rung by the SOUND MIXER and a red light goes on outside the door of the SOUND STAGE as a signal that all activity around the SET is to stop and no one is to come on or off the stage. This happens every time the camera rolls. When shooting on LOCATION there is no red light, but the bell is still sounded to warn everyone that a SHOT is about to begin. When the take is finished, the bell sounds twice for *all clear*.

ON-CALL
An actor, or CREW member, who may or may not be used the next day, but must remain available.

ON CAMERA
Any person or object that is seen by the camera while filming or taping.

ONE-LIGHT PRINT
An un-GRADED print made with a single light setting, to be used as a WORK PRINT only.

ONE SHEET
A movie poster.

ONE SHOT *(aka SINGLE)*
A shot showing a single person.

OPAQUE
Impenetrable by light. The opposite is transparent or translucent.

OPEN UP
1) To increase the size of the LENS APERTURE, and therefore let in more light, decreasing the DEPTH OF FIELD. 2) A term used when describing the translation of a play into a film. The story is no longer subject to the confines of a stage when it is put on film, so it "opens up" into the larger scope of the real world.

OPERATOR
See CAMERA OPERATOR.

115

OPTICAL HOUSE
A LABORATORY that specializes in OPTICAL EFFECTS and OPTICAL PRINTING.

OPTICAL PRINT
A print made by any means other than CONTACT PRINTING. This is done in an OPTICAL HOUSE. *See WET GATE.*

OPTICAL PRINTER
A special combination CAMERA and PROJECTOR capable of reproducing IMAGES on previously processed film, adding images, enlarging or reducing images *(i.e., SPECIAL EFFECTS, TITLES, SUPERIMPOSITIONS, etc.)* New images are exposed with the existing images onto new printing STOCK by the printer light. The newly exposed RAW STOCK now contains both images. Many special effects SCENES using MATTE SHOTS are printed in this manner.

OPTICALS *(aka OPTICAL EFFECTS)*
Any effect created with an OPTICAL PRINTER. *See DISSOLVE, EFFECTS, FADE, WIPE, MATTE SHOT.*

OPTICAL SOUND TRACK
Sound track reproduced on photographic film by optical means that creates sound when read by an optical sound reader, as opposed to magnetic sound track which is recorded on magnetic tape or film. The sound is reproduced by light waves, electronically converted to sound impulses during projection.

OPTION
An agreement in which a prospective buyer, for a fee, has exclusive rights to represent (develop, sell, etc.) a property or one's services for a specific period of time. Technically, an option is merely an offer to enter into a contract, but the potential seller cannot revoke the offer during the option term, because the potential buyer (option holder) has paid for it.

ORIGINAL
Usually refers to original NEGATIVE.

ORIGINAL SCREENPLAY
A screenplay written especially as a movie, and not adapted from another medium *(e.g., novel, short story, play).*

ORCHESTRATION
The art of SCORING for different instruments from a musical sketch.

ORCHESTRATOR
The person who takes the COMPOSER'S or ARRANGER'S sketch and assigns parts to the various voices and/or instruments. Sometimes the composer does his/her own ORCHESTRATIONS.

OS
Abbreviation for OFF SCREEN.

OSCAR
The nickname of the statuette given annually during the ACADEMY AWARDS ceremonies for outstanding achievement in various areas of the film industry. Although no one knows exactly how Oscar got his name, the most popular legend is that Margaret Herrick, the Academy librarian at the time, exclaimed upon seeing the statuette, "Why he looks just like my Uncle Oscar!" The newspapers and wire services picked up the quote and the name stuck. Other versions attribute the naming to Bette Davis and columnist Sidney Skolsky.

OUT OF FRAME
1) Anything outside the camera's field of view. 2) Threading the film wrong in the PROJECTOR (or having a poorly positioned projector GATE), causing part of two frames, or not the correct, centered part of one frame to be seen out the screen.

OUT OF SYNC
Picture and sound that are not coinciding properly. *See IN SYNC, SYNCHRONIZATION.*

OUTTAKES
FOOTAGE shot, but not selected for the final cut of a film, sometimes quite comical. Hal Needham's trademark has been to splice these together and run them during the END CREDITS of his movies.

OVERAGES *(aka COST OVERRUNS)*
Production costs that exceed the amount in the prepared BUDGET.

OVERCRANK
To run the camera at a speed faster than normal (24 FPS) producing SLOW MOTION. The opposite is UNDERCRANK, which produces ACCELERATED MOTION. The terms come from the days when motion picture cameras were HAND CRANKED.

OVERDEVELOPED
Negative film developted for a longer than normal period of time, or in a warmer than normal solution, causing the film to become extremely contrasty.

OVEREXPOSURE
1) When film has been exposed to too much light for proper exposure. 2) When an actor has been given too much publicity so the public gets tired of him or her.

OVERHEAD
The fixed costs of maintaining offices, facilities and personnel for a STUDIO or individual PRODUCTION/ PRODUCTION COMPANY. In the case of a studio, these costs are passed on the production companies or PRODUCERS renting facilities as a percentage of their BUDGETS.

OVERHEAD CLUSTERS
Suspended groups of large numbers of lights.

OVERHEAD SHOT
A shot where the camera sees the action from above.

OVERHEAD STRIPS
Suspended lighting units that light a broad area.

OVERLAP
1) The term refers to any situation in which the EFFECTS from one SEQUENCE are extended into the next for CONTINUITY purposes. Also meaning the extra FOOTAGE at the end of a SHOT for transitional use. 2) In sound, a SCENE in which one actor speaks over another actor's lines by accident or intentionally, or when a sound is carried over between shots.

OVERRUNS, COST
Un-BUDGETED, unexpected additional expenditures.

OVERSCALE
1) Fees that are above UNION minimums. 2) Objects or SETS that are larger than life.

OVER-THE-SHOULDER SHOT
A shot where the action is seen from a point directly behind (and to the left or right) an actor's head, with part of that actor's head and shoulder in the FRAME.

OVERSHOOT
To shoot too much FOOTAGE for necessary COVERAGE of a SCENE. This is a very costly practice, although not always as costly as UNDERSHOOTING, which entails going back and reshooting, perhaps having to re-build SETS, etc.

P

PA
Abbreviation for PRODUCTION ASSISTANT *(aka GOFER, RUNNER)*. This is now a UNION (DGA) position.

PACING
The rate or rhythm of theme development in a film, or of the DIALOGUE or action in an individual SCENE. Sometimes having a SCRIPT TIMED beforehand will help to find pacing problems that can be corrected before shooting starts. *See also SCRIPT TIMING.*

PACKAGE
To put together various elements (SCRIPT, DIRECTOR, ACTORS, PRODUCER, etc.) which make a film project saleable. Sometimes certain AGENTS/agencies specialize in packaging, using several of their own clients, providing the optimum number of agent's fees they can collect from the project.

PAN
1) The horizontal (side to side) movement of the camera on the axis of its TRIPOD or CAMERA MOUNT. *See also TILT.* 2) Bad reviews *(e.g., such-and-such film was panned in the TRADES).*

PANACLEAR
A rain or spray deflector made by PANAVISION, with a two-foot diameter, that mounts in front of the LENS and spins to keep water off of the lens.

PANAGLIDE
Trade name for a BODY FRAME for a motion picture camera developed by PANAVISION. It allows smooth, steady movement of a HAND-HELD camera. *See also STEADICAM.*

PAN AND TILT
A special fitting on the TRIPOD that allows the camera to PAN (move horizontally) or TILT (move vertically).

PANAVISION
Trademark of a motion picture camera system often used in shooting FEATURE FILMS. It is a WIDE SCREEN process using 35mm film and an ANAMORPHIC LENS. Panavision 70 (Super Panavision) uses 65mm film and an anamorphic lens. The 65mm film is used in the camera for shooting, while RELEASE PRINTS are on 70mm film. The extra 5mm are for the magnetic sound stripe on the edge.

PANAVISION 70 WITH TODD A-O SOUND
A 65mm unsqueezed NEGATIVE printed on 70mm film STOCK. The extra 5mm are for additional STEREOPHONIC MAGNETIC SOUND TRACKS (i.e., in addition to the normal OPTICAL SOUND TRACK) on either side of the PERFORATIONS. There are five SPROCKET HOLES per FRAME in this film as opposed to the four in 35mm film.

PANCHROMATIC
Black and white film that is sensitive to all colors visible to the human eye.

PAN GLASS
Used primarily by the DIRECTOR or DIRECTOR OF PHOTO - GRAPHY, this blue-green or brown-yellow FILTER allows the viewer to see approximately what the SCENE will look like when shot.

PARALLAX
The difference in FRAMING between an object seen by the camera and the object seen by the viewer through a separate VIEWFINDER. This phenomenon is more noticeable in CLOSE-UPS and must be adjusted for. A through-the-LENS viewing system avoids the problem.

PARALLEL
A platform used to raise the camera and CAMERA CREW above the floor of the SET or LOCATION in order to take high angle shots. Oftentimes, lights are placed on the parallels.

PARALLEL ACTION
Action in two different SCENES which, by INTERCUTTING (CROSSCUTTING), takes place concurrently.

PARI PASSU
Pro rata and concurrent. Literally, with equal progress side by side. Used most often to describe the relationship of investors and profit participants in a film vis-a-vis RECOUPMENT of their investment, payment of deferments, or PROFITS. To determine the total obligation owed to the entire category entitled to pari passu payments, in turn requires the determination of the respective rights of each individual member of the category. The payment is calculated by applying the fraction-obligation to payee/obligations to entire category to the fund available. For illustration, assume that two investors are pari passu, that each has invested $100,000, but one has bargained for 10% interest, and the other for 12%. After one year, $100,000 is available to be paid for recoupment. The calculation for the 10% investor would be $110,000 (principal and interest)/$222,000 (total principal and interest) X $100,000 = $49,549.55.

PASSING SHOT
A shot where either the camera is stationary and the subject moves, or the subject is stationary and and the camera moves. This differs from PAN or TILT as the camera does not follow the action. *See also DRIVE-BY, RUN-BY.*

PANEL/PATCH PANEL
An electrical board that contains the necessary connections for the electrical equipment on a PRODUCTION.

PAY OR PLAY
A contractual obligation which guarantees the employer will pay the employee whether or not the services are performed or required. This

kind of GUARANTEE is usually given only to high-level people in the industry (STARS, DIRECTORS, WRITERS, etc.) and, in some cases, may be a DEAL BREAKER during negotiations if not agreed to.

PENCIL TEST
Un-inked ANIMATION CELLS (before the picture has been colored in) which are photographed to see if the movement is correct.

PER DIEM
A specific amount of money calculated on a daily basis to cover costs incurred by the member of the company while shooting on LOCATION. Such costs can include meals, lodging, laundry, etc. Travel costs are usually additional.

PERFORATIONS *(aka SPROCKET HOLES, abbr. PERFS)*
The regularly and equally spaced holes, four per FRAME in 35mm, punched on the edges of motion picture film. In most 16mm film, there is only one side with perforations. POSITIVE film (PRINT) perfs are usually stronger than those on NEGATIVE film in order to withstand the strain of multiple PROJECTIONS.

PERFORMER
Any actor in a PRODUCTION who has a speaking, dancing or singing part. EXTRAS or WALK-ONS are not considered performers. *See also FEATURED PLAYER, SUPPORTING PLAYER.*

PERK
Short for perquisite. FRINGE BENEFIT. Privilege or profit over and above a salary. There are many perks in the film business, used as incentives for people to take a job, or to keep them in a job *(i.e., cars, expense accounts, WARDROBE from films, etc.)* Often perks are not left to Fate, but are written into contracts.

PERSISTENCE OF VISION
The human eye retains an IMAGE briefly after it disappears. This phenomenon allows the illusion of movement when still images are projected at the rate of 16 or more FRAMES PER SECOND.

PG
Parental Guidance suggested. *See RATING, MPAA.*

PG 13
Children under the age of 13 not admitted to the theater without a parent or guardian. This is a relatively new rating introduced in 1984. *See RATING, MPAA.*

PHOTO DOUBLE
A DOUBLE who very closely resembles, or is made to resemble the actor whom he is doubling. *See also STUNT DOUBLE, DOUBLE.*

PHOTOFLOOD
A high intensity incandescent tungsten bulb. A side effect of over-loading the voltage to produce high intensity light is a shorter bulb life.

PHOTOMETER
Similar to a LIGHT METER, this piece of equipment accurately measures brightness.

PICK-UP
1) SCENES or SHOTS filmed after the completion of PRINCIPAL PHOTOGRAPHY, to fill any gaps in CONTINUITY. 2) Decision by a STUDIO to take on a project. 3) Decision by a NETWORK that a PILOT will become a SERIES, or that an existing series will continue. 4) To shoot a portion of a shot that has already been made in order to get a different reading on a particular line, or to make some other small change in a performance without going back to the beginning of the shot. This is called a PRINT AND PICK UP.

PICTURE DUPLICATE NEGATIVE
See DUPLICATE NEGATIVE.

PICTURE NEGATIVE *(aka NEGATIVE)*
The resulting film with IMAGE after the exposed film has been DEVELOPED in the LAB. See ORIGINAL.

PICTURE PRINT *(aka SILENT PRINT)*
PROCESSED film with a positive IMAGE and no SOUND TRACK.

PICTURE RELEASE NEGATIVE
Negative which has been CONFORMED to the WORK PRINT, from which RELEASE PRINTS are STRUCK.

PILOT
Usually a 90 minute or 2-hour Movie Of the Week (MOW) that is the forerunner of a TV series. For example, the pilot of the series *KOJAK* was *THE MARCUS-NELSON MURDERS.*

PILOT PINS *(aka REGISTER PINS)*
The stationary teeth in the GATE of a camera (PRINTER or PROJECTOR) that fit into the SPROCKET HOLES (or PERFORATIONS) of the film as it advances, and keeps the film in place.

PINCUSHION DISTORTION
An ABERRATION in a LENS causes this aptly named distortion which causes normally square IMAGES on the film to curve inward.

PITCH
On motion picture film, the distance between two successive SPROCKET HOLES (or PERFORATIONS).

PLAY (n.)
1) The book, usually divided into acts and scenes, containing DIALOGUE and a few stage directions, upon which a theatrical presentation is based. 2) A theatrical presentation using actors in front of a live audience.

PLAY (v.)
To work well *(e.g., "This SCENE will play.")*

PLAYBACK
Music and/or vocals that were previously recorded, used when shooting musical numbers.

PLOT
The main story line which usually can be described in a very few words.

PLOT POINT
A turning point in the action of a SCREENPLAY.

POC
Abbreviation for PRODUCTION OFFICE COORDINATOR.

POINT
The percentage, or fraction thereof, of the PROFITS (NET or GROSS) of a motion picture or television project. Points are usually negotiated as part of a DIRECTOR'S DEAL and sometimes as part of a WRITER'S or ACTOR'S deal, depending upon their clout. If a STAR can command it, his/her points may be based on gross profits rather than the usual net profits.

POINT OF VIEW (SHOT) *(Abbr. POV)*
A shot filmed so that it appears to be seen from a particular character's point of view. In general, point of view means seeing out of someone's eyes.

POLAROID FILTER *(aka POLA SCREEN)*
A filter that helps eliminate reflections and glare.

POLECAT
A support for lamps.

POLISH
A slight revision of a SCRIPT. This is a special classification recognized by the WRITERS GUILD OF AMERICA with a specific and separate pay scale. If a polish becomes too extensive, it is called a REVISION.

POLYVISION
A forerunner of CINERAMA, Abel Gance developed this triple-screen projection system in 1927 for his historic film, NAPOLEON.

POSITIVE
A print made from a NEGATIVE (or STOCK shot in the camera with REVERSAL FILM) with the proper colors appearing in their proper places.

POST-PRODUCTION
The time, after PRODUCTION, when EDITING, LOOPING, SCORING, INSERTS, FOLEY, MIXING, etc., are done. In other words, everything you need to finish the film.

POST-SYNCHRONIZATION
The act of re-recording DIALOGUE or sound in a proper acoustical environment. Used when sound has been recorded unsatisfactorily at the time of shooting, or when it was impossible to record the sounds/dialogue concurrently while shooting. Also used to translate the dialogue from one language to another. *See also DUBBING, LOOPING, ADR.*

POT
See DIAL.

PRACTICAL
Refers to a PROP or piece of SET DRESSING that actually works, *(e.g., a shower, a door lock, a gun.)* Also a light on a SET that works.

PRE-MIX *(aka PRE-DUB)*
An early stage in creating a COMPOSITE TRACK. Several SOUND TRACKS are combined to make the eventual final mix simpler.

PRE-PRODUCTION
The period of preparation before PRINCIPAL PHOTOGRAPHY begins. This involves preparing the SCRIPT, SCRIPT BREAK - DOWN, BUDGET, LOCATION SCOUTING, COSTUME design, SET construction, etc. In other words, everything you need to do in order to shoot a film.

PREQUEL
The FEATURE FILM, television film or television episode that is released (or aired) after the original but actually tells a story that happened before the original *(e.g., the SCENES with Robert DeNiro as young Vito Corleone in THE GODFATHER, PART II, were considered a prequel to THE GODFATHER.)*

PRE-SCORING
The preparation of the musical SCORE before a film is shot. The standard process is to compose, ARRANGE, and record the MUSIC TRACK after completion of shooting.

PRESSURE PLATE
The plate behind the APERTURE of the projector (or camera or printer) that holds the film snugly in place.

PRESS AGENT
See PUBLICIST.

PRESS JUNKET
A trip arranged by the PUBLIC RELATIONS DEPARTMENT wherein several members of the press are sent on LOCATION for the purpose of interviewing the CAST, DIRECTOR, PRODUCER, etc., or a trip made by the CAST, DIRECTOR, etc. when the film is RELEASED to publicize the picture. Since this is an expensive proposition, press junkets are usually reserved for big BUDGET PRODUCTIONS that want a lot of advance publicity.

PRESS KIT
A package of materials, *(e.g., copies of reviews, 8 X 10 stills from the film, color transparencies, press releases)* that are sent to various members of the press to encourage them to write about a particular film. The materials are put together by the UNIT PUBLICIST and the

PUBLIC RELATIONS DEPARTMENT. Fairly new are the electronic press kits that put together TRAILERS and/or interviews with key people from the production to be shown on TV (usually CABLE).

PREVIEW
An advance showing of a film before the scheduled release date. Previews are either shown to invited groups (press, industry executives, friends, etc.) to help spread good word of mouth, or to the paying public as a test. It is not unusual for changes to be made after a preview. Many DIRECTORS have the contractual right to a preview or two before submitting their final EDITED version. *See also SNEAK PREVIEW.*

PRIMARY COLORS
In terms of color photography, there are two ways to create colors. The first, the additive method, takes colored lights and, by combining them, creates the desired color. The second, the subtractive method, starts with white light (all the colors of the light spectrum combined in motion) and, by FILTERING out (or subtracting) leaves the desired color.

The primary additive colors are red-orange, green and blue-violet which, when mixed, produce white light. Varying the proportions of the mixture will produce all the other colors. The primary subtractive colors are CYAN (blue-green), yellow and magenta (purple-pink), which are the complementary colors to the additive primary colors. The subtractive primary colors absorb the red, green and blue wavelengths, thus subtracting them from the white light. When mixed, they can produce any color in the spectrum, even black (having absorbed all colors of light).

Early color cinematography was based on the additive process, but today it is based on the subtractive process which, even though it requires chemical processing, is more practical. The additive and subtractive primary colors have to do with light. The primary colors in painting (colors from pigment) are red, yellow and blue.

PRIME LENS
An individual lens of a specific FOCAL LENGTH, as opposed to a ZOOM LENS, which has variable focal lengths.

PRINCIPAL PHOTOGRAPHY
That segment of time during which all scripted material covering all the speaking parts is filmed. SECOND UNIT material may be shot at approximately the same time. It is possible, however, that second unit can be shot either before or after principal photography.

PRINCIPAL PLAYERS
Those members of the CAST who are the main featured actors in the film or television show.

PRINT (n.)
A POSITIVE made from an ORIGINAL (or DUPE) NEGATIVE, used for PROJECTION.

PRINT (v.)
A LAB process of creating a POSITIVE from a NEGATIVE, or a negative from a positive. By using a special REVERSAL PRINTING process, the lab can also produce positives from positives and negatives from negatives. *See also CRI.*

PRINT AND PICK UP
To shoot a portion of a SHOT that has already been made in order to get a different reading on a particular line, or to make some other small change in a PERFORMANCE without going back to the beginning of the shot.

PRINTER
A device which makes PRINTS (or other GENERATIONS) from POSITIVES or negatives. The two main types of printers are the OPTICAL PRINTER, which projects the IMAGE onto RAW STOCK for reproduction, and the CONTACT PRINTER, in which the original film is placed in physical contact (contacted) with the raw stock and exposed to light. There are also two methods of printing: Step Printing, in which the film is advanced intermittently, with each FRAME being stationary during exposure; and Continuous-Motion printing, in which the raw stock and original continuously move during exposure.

PRINTER LIGHT
A control on the PRINTER which, when adjusted during PROCESSING, can correct any differences in the density of the NEGATIVE.

PRINT IT!
The DIRECTOR'S order after a good TAKE (noted on the CAMERA REPORT and in the SCRIPT SUPERVISOR'S log) that when the SHOT is PROCESSED, a positive PRINT (WORK PRINT) should be made.

PROCESS BODY

A specially-designed, simulated vehicle (car, train, etc.) whose front and sides can be removed so that the vehicle's interior can be photographed. Usually used for PROCESS SHOTS.

PROCESSING

A term used for DEVELOPING and PRINTING film.

PROCESS SHOT

Used primarily for moving automobile or train shots, the previously-filmed BACKGROUND of the shot is PROJECTED through a transparent SCREEN, while the actors sit in the PROCESS BODY and perform. *See BACK PROJECTION, REAR PROJECTION.*

PRODUCER

Ideally, the first person on a project and the last person off. The producer's role is to find and develop a project, hire the WRITER/s and develop the SCRIPT, hire the DIRECTOR, ACTORS, etc., arrange for FINANCING, oversee the PRODUCTION, on this and any other projects he or she may be producing concurrently. (In episodic television, this person is called the EXECUTIVE PRODUCER.) Also, the producer may be involved in the RELEASE and EXPLOITATION of the film. Some directors and actors who initiate their own projects act as their own producer. *See HYPHENATE.*

PRODUCER'S NET PROFITS

See PROFITS.

PRODUCTION

1) A film or television show in the works. 2) The period of time during which a film or television show is shot and EDITING commences.

PRODUCTION ASSISTANT

(Abbr. PA, aka GOFER, RUNNER)
An entry-level member of the PRODUCTION CREW, whose job it is to do small, but necessary jobs for the PRODUCER, DIRECTOR, PRODUCTION MANAGER, PRODUCTION OFFICE COORDINATOR, etc.

PRODUCTION AUDITOR

(aka LOCATION AUDITOR, LOCATION ACCOUNTANT)
That member of the Production Staff whose primary responsibility is to maintain up-to-date, accurate financial records of the costs entailed in the production of the film or television show. This position may be

covered by a UNION. The Production Auditor works directly with the PRODUCTION MANAGER and the financing entity.

PRODUCTION BOARD
See PRODUCTION STRIP BOARD.

PRODUCTION BREAKDOWN
See BREAKDOWN.

PRODUCTION COMPANY
An organization created for, or responsible for the development and realization of a film or television project.

PRODUCTION DESIGNER
See ART DIRECTOR.

PRODUCTION MANAGER
See UNIT PRODUCTION MANAGER.

PRODUCTION NUMBER
A number in a film or television show with music, dancing and/or singing. It is a small production within the production. There are usually special SETS and COSTUMES for the number.

PRODUCTION OFFICE COORDINATOR *(Abbr. POC)*
A clerical member of the production staff who works directly for the PRODUCTION MANAGER and acts as a liaison between the Production Office and all other groups during the production. In some parts of the United States, this is a UNION position.

PRODUCTION REPORT
A daily report itemizing all elements used for that particular day's (or night's) SHOOTING. It is filled out by the KEY SECOND ASSISTANT DIRECTOR and submitted to the PRODUCTION MANAGER for approval. It is then sent to the PRODUCER, DIRECTOR, PRODUCTION AUDITOR, the STUDIO (if any), and any other party concerned with the daily costs of the production. The report includes such items as: the SCENES shot, the number of pages completed, amount of FOOTAGE exposed, any abnormalities that would explain any OVERAGE or UNDERAGE of material covered, any penalties incurred and their reasons, which CREW members and actors were used, etc.

PRODUCTION STRIP BOARD
A scheduling tool used by PRODUCTION MANAGERS and FIRST ASSISTANT DIRECTORS in determining exactly how much time it will take to SHOOT the film, and who is needed for each SCENE. Each scene in the script is marked on a separate strip according to whether it is an Interior or Exterior, Day or Night. These strips are then laid out on the board, which consists of many panels, arranged to show the most efficient and least expensive order in which to shoot the project.

PRODUCTION VALUE
The synergistic combination of the quality of certain elements in a film such as PRODUCTION DESIGN, scenery (locale), COSTUMES, LIGHTING and sound, that add perceived value to the film without necessarily increasing the BUDGET. Films may have high production value without substance.

PROFITS
Profits, NET and GROSS, defy definition. Such terms are redefined in every industry contract dealing with earnings participation. Although some companies have adopted standard, or their own customary definitions, the definitions are still subject to negotiation. Two issues determine each specific definition: 1) what income is included and accountable, and 2) what deductions may be taken against that income before applying the participant's percentage to the remainder. Many in the industry are cynical about deriving real profits from a picture's earnings, hence, a prospective participant is well advised to seek skilled and experienced, industry-wise counsel when negotiating profits.

PROJECTION
1) The ability to make one's voice carry a great distance. 2) The act of running a film through a PROJECTOR, whose beam of light throws the IMAGE, many times enlarged, onto a screen. 3) Forecasts about a film's performance at the BOX OFFICE and any revenue-gathering markets. *See also BACK SCREEN PROJECTION, BLUE SCREEN PROJECTION.*

PROJECTION BOOTH
A small room in the back of the theater from which the IMAGE is projected onto the SCREEN.

PROJECTIONIST
The person who operates the PROJECTOR, usually a member of IATSE.

PROJECTION PRINTER
See OPTICAL PRINTER.

PROJECTION SYNC
The spacing between the SOUND TRACK and its corresponding picture: 20 FRAMES ahead of the picture for 35mm, 26 frames ahead for 16mm.

PROJECTOR
A light-producing device that throws filmed IMAGES onto a SCREEN. When the images are projected at a rapid enough rate (24 FPS), the illusion of motion is created. *See PERSISTENCE OF VISION.*

PROP
Abbreviation for PROPERTY. Any moveable item seen or used on a motion picture SET and used in a particular SCENE. For example, the gun that Michael Caine uses in DEATHTRAP to "kill" Christopher Reeve is a prop, while the guns in the collection on the wall are part of the SET DRESSING. The lines between props and set dressing do sometimes overlap.

PROPERTY
1) See PROP. 2) Any idea, novel, short story, magazine article, SCREENPLAY, etc., that is the basis for a motion picture.

PROP PERSON/ PROPERTY MASTER
The person responsible for maintenance, availability and placement of all props on a SET.

PROP MAKER
A member of the construction department *(i.e., carpenter)* who is responsible for making the necessary props for a film. Should not be confused with PROP MASTER.

PROPERTY SHEET
List and schedule of all props to be used in the film.

PROTECTION MASTER
See INTERPOSITIVE, MASTER POSITIVE, CRI.

PUBLICIST
The person responsible for promotion and publicity of a person, place, or thing through radio, television, newspapers, magazines, etc. The aim of the publicity is to make the client more well-known and, hopefully, a more desirable commodity. The person who oversees all publicity is

called Publicity Director. On a film project, the publicist is called UNIT PUBLICIST. This is also a UNION position and covered by the PUBLICISTS GUILD. *See also PRESS AGENT.*

PUBLICITY STILL
A still photograph taken before, during or after PRINCIPAL PHOTOGRAPHY of a motion picture to be used in publicizing the movie.

PULLBACK
Backwards movement of the camera from a CLOSE SHOT to a MEDIUM or LONG SHOT (or from medium to long shot, etc.)

PULL FOCUS
A semi-arty type of SHOT in which an object in the FOREGROUND is out of focus and an object in the BACKGROUND is in focus (or vice versa), then the focus is switched so that the foreground is in focus and the background is fuzzy (or vice versa).

PUP
A small focused light source of 500-watts.

PUSH *(aka FORCE DEVELOP)*
To PROCESS film as if it had a higher (more sensitive) ASA rating *(e.g., 100 ASA at 200 or 400 ASA)*. The resulting IMAGE will be grainier but, in some instances (low-light conditions, for example), it may be the only way to get the SHOT.

Q

QUARTER APPLE
A box that is the same width and length as an APPLE BOX, but only one-quarter the height.

QUARTER LOAD
One-quarter the amount of explosive material used by SPECIAL EFFECTS in guns and explosive devides for smaller explosions. *See HALF LOAD.*

QUARTZ LIGHT
A light that uses a quartz bulb around the filament.

QUICK CUT
See JUMP CUT.

QUIET ON THE SET!
The traditional command issued by the AD, used to call the CAST and CREW to order before the order, "roll camera!" is given. This keeps order on the set during waiting time between TAKES, when the noise level makes it difficult for the DIRECTOR and actors to concentrate.

R

R
Restricted (RATING). Children under the age of 17 are not admitted to the theater without a parent or guardian. *See MPAA, RATING.*

RACK
1) Archaic term for threading film in a MOVIOLA, KEM or other viewing device - or PROJECTOR. 2) To line up a FRAME in the GATE on a camera, projector or EDITING machine. 3) Shorthand command given by the DP to the OPERATOR to adjust the focus to pre-determined positions. *See RACK FOCUS.*

RACK FOCUS
To adjust the LENS during a SHOT so that the subject is IN FOCUS.

RACKOVER
A feature of the early motion picture cameras that allowed the entire film mechanism to shift to one side so that the OPERATOR could see through the LENS during REHEARSAL. The lens had to be racked back into position before SHOOTING. These days, cameras have through-the-lens viewing systems.

RAILS
1) Scaffolds high above the SET where lamps are mounted for overhead lighting. 2) DOLLY TRACKS.

RAIN EFFECT
To simulate rain on a SET (indoors or out), hoses, perforated pipes and sprinkler systems are used. There are several systems: the Rain Standard is the most common. It is a sprinkler head that has been mounted on a moveable stanchion about 25 feet above the set or actors. Rain Clusters are systems of sprinklers used to cover large areas. For a more realistic look, sometimes it is necessary to drench the entire area beforehand so that there are puddles, and apply a glossy material to the ground and walls. It is also possible to add rain (or snow) to a dry scene after it has been shot by OPTICALLY SUPERIMPOSING STOCK FOOTAGE of rain (or snow) over the SCENE. In this case, the actors' clothing should be pre-soaked.

RAMP
1) A slanted platform used to move a DOLLY alongside actors as they travel across an uneven surface or up and down levels. 2) A piece of equipment used by a STUNTPERSON to allow a moving object (a person, vehicle, etc.) to pass above another object.

RANK CINTEL
Trademarked name for the machine which performs the film-to-tape process known as TELECINE.

RATING, MPAA
The MOTION PICTURE ASSOCIATION OF AMERICA'S established system of categorizing FEATURE FILMS according to viewer audience suitability. The categories are as follows: G - General Audiences, PG - Parental Guidance suggested, PG 13 - Children under the age of 13 are not admitted without a parent or guardian, R - Restricted, children under the age of 17 not admitted without parent or guardian, and X - No one under 21 allowed. The MPAA also rates TRAILERS. There are two ratings: All Audience and Restricted. A Restricted trailer may only play with an R- or X- rated film.

RATIO
See ASPECT RATIO, SHOOTING RATIO.

RAW STOCK
Unexposed and unprocessed film.

REACTION SHOT
A shot, usually a CLOSE-UP, of a person reacting to something said or done in a previous shot or OFF CAMERA.

READ
1) To register on a LIGHT METER *(i.e., "will (an IMAGE) read?")*
2) To register to the eye - whether an object will be noticeable on
SCREEN *(i.e., "is that sign too small to read on film?")* 3) In the
case of a SCENE in a SCRIPT, to play smoothly and coherently. 4) To
AUDITION an actor for a part.

READER
A Story Department employee (or an employee of an agency, a
PRODUCER, etc.) whose job it is to read, summarize and write an
opinion on material submitted to the STUDIO or PRODUCTION
COMPANY, etc., for consideration. Their resulting analysis is called
COVERAGE.

READING
1) A measurement of available light (e.g., to take a light reading). 2)
An AUDITION. 3) The verbal part of a performance *(e.g., "I liked the
reading in TAKE 3 the best").*

REALISATEUR
French term for DIRECTOR. *See also METTEUR-EN-SCENE.*

REAR SCREEN PROJECTION
A system of projecting film onto the back of a translucent SCREEN -
as opposed to the front of the screen as in standard projection. Although
it is sometimes (though rarely) used in theaters, its main use is in
PRODUCTION, as an exterior BACKGROUND more easily shot in a
STUDIO. For example, a SHOT in which two characters are driving in
a car. Out of the car's window we see scenery (streets, buildings, trees,
mountains, etc.) passing by. The LIVE ACTION is shot in the studio
against the projected background (STOCK FOOTAGE, or footage shot
by a SECOND UNIT), making sure that the camera and projector are
carefully SYNCHED to prevent flickering. This is referred to as a
PROCESS SHOT. For extremely large scenes, the more complex
MATTE SHOT (or TRAVELLING MATTE) is used.

RECORDING
The technique of putting live or previously recorded sound or IMAGE
on magnetic tape. *See MIX.*

RECORDIST *(aka PRODUCTION MIXER)*
The CREW member responsible for recording sound during
PRODUCTION. During POST PRODUCTION, the mixer is
responsible for mixing SOUND TRACKS into the final COMPOSITE

TRACK, which is then put onto the film, either on an OPTICAL TRACK, or MAGNETIC STRIPE.

RECOUPMENT
Recovery of one's investment.

RE-DRESS
To change the look of a SET. *See DRESS.*

REDUCTION PRINT
A print made from a wider gauged ORIGINAL, for example, a 16mm print made from a 35mm original. The opposite is BLOW-UP.

REEL
For projection and storage purposes, motion picture film is wound on metal or plastic wheels (reels). The standard size reel (35mm) can hold 1000 feet (10 minutes) of film - but rarely holds over 900 feet. More common now are double reels that hold 2000 feet of film. The 10 minute reel became such a standard that people still refer to a film length in terms of the number of (1000 foot) reels. It also refers to the film on the reel as in, "a SCENE located in the first reel of the picture."

REFLECTED LIGHT
Illumination bounced off the subject being photographed. *See also EXPOSURE METER.*

REFLECTOR
A reflective panel, usually made of silver or gold flake material, used to direct light where it is needed. Sometimes white cards, called BOUNCE BOARDS, made of cardboard or foam core, are used as reflectors.

REFLEX CAMERA
A camera that, through a system of mirrors, permits through-the-LENS viewing while shooting. This system eliminates the PARALLAX problem.

REGISTRATION PINS *(aka PILOT PINS)*
The stationary teeth in the film GATE of a camera or PROJECTOR which fit into the SPROCKET HOLES and pull the film down to advance it.

RELEASE
1) To put a motion picture into general or limited DISTRIBUTION.
2) To dismiss *(e.g., an actor after his/her work has been completed for the day.)* 3) To free from contractual obligation *(i.e., to give the axe,*

to show the door). 4) (Press) A notice sent out by the publicity department. 5) A legal document giving the PRODUCTION COMPANY permission to include the likeness of a person who has been photographed in a film or video to be exhibited.

RELEASE NEGATIVE
A MASTER negative for making RELEASE PRINTS.

RELEASE PRINT
A final COMPOSITE PRINT ready for DISTRIBUTION to theaters.

REMAKE
A new version of a previously-made film. The Judy Garland/James Mason, and the Barbra Streisand/Kris Kristofferson versions of *A STAR IS BORN* were both remakes of the original 1937 Janet Gaynor/Fredric March version. *BREATHLESS,* with Richard Gere, was a remake of Goddard's *AU BOUT DE SOUFFLE,* and both *DOWN AND OUT IN BEVERLY HILLS* and Gene Kelly's *GIGOT,* were remakes of Jean Renoir's *BOUDU SAUVE DES EAUX.*

REPLAY *(aka PLAYBACK)*
1) To re-wind and re-run a SCENE, or just the audio or visual portion, in order to see if it has been recorded properly. 2) To re-run a musical piece during shooting so that the actors can dance, or react to, music which will be added later in the MIX.

REPORT SHEETS
Logs or data sheets filled out daily by the Camera and Sound departments listing each TAKE and noting which ones are to be printed and which ones are NG (no good).

REPORT TO
An instruction written on the CALL SHEET to indicate that CREW members are working at a STUDIO or at a local LOCATION, and that their work can begin upon their arrival at the SET.

RE-RECORD
Transfer of an audio or video track from one medium (film, tape, disk) to another. Also, the combining of many SOUND TRACKS in the final MIX.

RE-RELEASE
A film that is re-issued after having already been in some form of DISTRIBUTION (GENERAL or LIMITED) at an earlier date.

RESIDUALS
Additional compensation equivalent to an author's royalty, paid to ACTORS, DIRECTORS, etc., according to union contract. Not all union members receive residuals.

RESOLUTION *(aka RESOLVING POWER)*
The amount of detail capable of being recorded through a LENS onto film or tape.

RE-TAKE
To re-shoot a previously made SCENE that was unsatisfactory for one reason or another.

RE-VAMP
To re-arrange a SET for use in another SEQUENCE, or in another PRODUCTION.

REVEAL
A SHOT that opens up or pulls back to show something that wasn't previously visible.

REVERSAL DUPE
A duplicate POSITIVE made from a positive.

REVERSAL FILM
Film that is processed by the LAB directly into a POSITIVE (like slides in a still camera) or from a NEGATIVE into another negative.

REVERSE ACTION *(REVERSE MOTION)*
The technique of showing filmed action going backwards. Mainly used as a SPECIAL EFFECT.

REVERSE ANGLE SHOT/REVERSE
A shot taken from an angle almost 180 degrees opposite from the preceding shot. This is used frequently when two actors are talking facing each other, or when one actor is shown going through a doorway, or entering a room.

REVERSE SCENE
A scene that has been flipped during PRINTING so that the IMAGE looks reversed, as if it is reflected in a mirror.

REVISION
The re-writing step greater than a POLISH but less than the next DRAFT. This is a special classification recognized by the WRITERS

GUILD OF AMERICA with a specific and separate pay scale. Revisions to a SCREENPLAY made after it has been distributed to the actors and others connected with the PRODUCTION are usually printed on different colored paper with the date of the revision noted on the page. The color sequence of revised pages is: blue, pink, yellow, green, goldenrod and, if necessary, white again. *See also BLUE PAGES.*

REWIND (n.)
A geared device used to rewind film, consisting of two cranks with shafts: one for the feed REEL and one for the take-up reel. Electric rewinds are used in PROJECTION BOOTHS.

REWIND (v.)
To return film to its original REEL or onto a CORE using a REWIND.

RE-WRITES
See REVISIONS.

RIFLE MIKE
See SHOTGUN MIKE.

RIFLE SPOT
A SPOTLIGHT producing a long, slim beam of light.

RIGGERS
Those CREW members responsible for the construction of the scaffolding (aka RIGGING) on a SET, and the placement of the lights that go on the rigging.

RIGGING (n.)
Scaffolding.

RIGGING (v.)
The placement of STUDIO lights before shooting.

RIM LIGHT
A light used to produce a halo effect when it is placed behind the subject.

RISER
A stepped platform used to elevate actors, PROPS, etc.

RITTER
See WIND MACHINE.

ROLE
A part played by an actor or actress.

ROLL
A length of film on a CORE. The film can be any length.

ROLLING TITLE
(aka CRAWL, CREEPING TITLE or RUNNING TITLE)
Film CREDITS that roll from the bottom to the top of the SCREEN. Very rarely do you see rolling MAIN CREDITS, usually just rolling END CREDITS.

ROLL IT/ROLL CAMERA/ROLL PLEASE/ROLLING
What the FIRST ASSISTANT DIRECTOR says to the company to alert them that a TAKE is about to commence. This is the CUE for the camera and sound to start. When the camera is running the CAMERA OPERATOR says, *"Rolling"* and when the sound is running at the proper speed, the SOUND MAN says, *"Speed."* After this, the DIRECTOR calls, *"ACTION! "* and the take begins.

ROLL NUMBER
A number assigned to a roll of film, used for identification.

ROOM TONE
The existing presence or AMBIENCE in a quiet room, recorded onto a BUZZ TRACK, to be later MIXED in with the DIALOGUE TRACK, making a SCENE sound more realistic, and hides CUTS in the dialogue track.

ROSTER
The list of members available for work kept by various UNIONS and GUILDS.

ROSTRUM
A small base on folding legs upon which a camera or lighting unit may be mounted.

ROUGH CUT
The first stage of EDITING, in which all SCENES in the film are placed in their approximate order to tell the story. The FINE CUT is a long way off.

ROYALTY
A negotiated percentage of income based on sales. *See also RESIDUAL.*

RUN-BY
A SHOT in which a moving car (or other vehicle) travels past a stationary camera.

RUN LINES
To rehearse DIALOGUE - something that actors usually do before shooting a SCENE, so as to be well prepared.

RUNNERS
1) Scaffolding on which lights, backdrops and other equipment can be hung. 2) The PRODUCTION ASSISTANTS *(aka GOFER)* who run errands for the PRODUCER, DIRECTOR, PRODUCTION MANAGER, etc.

RUNNING SHOT
A shot in which a moving camera keeps pace with a moving object or person. *See TRACKING SHOT, DOLLY SHOT, TRAVELLING SHOT.*

RUNNING SPEED
The rate at which film runs through a camera or PROJECTOR, or which tape runs through a recorder or PLAYBACK machine. Running speed for film is measured in FRAMES PER SECOND and tape is measured in INCHES PER SECOND. *See FPS, IPS.*

RUNNING TIME
The total length of time required to project a film at its normal speed. Most FEATURE FILMS are between 85 and 110 minutes long.

RUN-OF-SHOW
A contractual term meaning that a certain person - usually a principal CAST member - has been hired for a specific salary for a specific number of weeks (the entire show), no matter how many days that actor works during that time. This is opposed to being hired on a daily or weekly basis.

RUN-THROUGH *(aka WALK-THROUGH)*
A complete rehearsal of actors (with or without equipment) without film running in the camera.

RUSHES
See DAILIES.

S

SAFE ACTION AREA
That portion of a film FRAME which will be visible when shown on television. *See also ASPECT RATIO*.

SAFETY BASE *(aka SAFETY FILM)*
A slow-burning film base (usually cellulose with acetate) which is non-combustive. Most films shot before 1950 used highly-flammable NITRATE BASE stock. Now, many old films have been transferred to safety base.

SAG
Abbreviation for SCREEN ACTORS GUILD.

SAMPLE PRINT
See CHECK PRINT.

SANDBAG
A standard piece of equipment found in all GRIP PACKAGES. It is a small, divided burlap or plastic bag filled with sand used to temporarily steady or hold down certain pieces of equipment. It is especially useful on windy days when shooting outside.

SATURATION
The measure of intensity of the color in a photographed IMAGE. Higher saturation gives richer, more vivid colors (*e.g., THE BLACK STALLION, THE NATURAL, BEING THERE, all shot by Caleb Deschanel*), while lower saturation (*aka DESATURATED*) results in subdued and more subtle colors. Many times desaturated colors are used to create certain effects (*e.g., the look of the dustbowl sequence shot by Haskell Wexler in Hal Asbhy's BOUND FOR GLORY*).

SCALE
The minimum wage established by each UNION or each individual job category. Usually, an experienced CREW member (or well-known actor) will receive more than scale.

SCALE PLUS TEN
A common practice, especially in regard to an actor's salary, in which the person is paid scale, plus an extra ten percent to cover the AGENT'S fee.

SCENARIO
Old term for SCREENPLAY. Most commonly used today to refer to PLOT or storyline.

SCENE
1) A scene may be a single SHOT or a series of shots that take place in a LOCATION, or present a main action or activity. 2) When BREAKING DOWN a SCRIPT, a scene can mean a unit of action or DIALOGUE which occurs in the same location at the same period of time. Each scene has its own number. Generally, a scene number will not change if an actor enters or leaves the scene, but this rule is not absolute.

SCENE DOCK
The area where FLATS for SETS are stored.

SCENE NAME
The identification describing the location of the action of the scene or the action itself (*e.g., Amy's Room, the Knife Throwing scene*).

SCENERY
Any part of a SET that gives the illusion of a locale.

SCENIC ARTIST
The person who paints the murals or BACKGROUNDS on the SET. Scenic artists also touch up and age sets and objects used in the film. They usually precede the CREW onto a LOCATION to PREP.

SCOOP
A WIDE-ANGLE floodlight.

SCORE (n.)
The musical accompaniment to a film.

SCORE (v.)
To compose music for a specific film.

SCORING STAGE
A SOUND STAGE for a large number of musicians, with facilities for SCREENING a film while the music is being recorded.

SCRAPER
A device, used with a HOT SPLICER, for removing the EMULSION from the film before cementing the SPLICE.

SCRATCHES
Deep grooves on the surface of film caused by poor or too frequent projection, improper handling, or camera friction. Scratches are more serious than ABRASIONS, in that they are deeper and often damage the EMULSION.

SCRATCH PRINT *(aka SLOP PRINT)*
A print STRUCK from WORK PRINT, usually made to meet a deadline, or to allow the EDITOR to send one print to the NEGATIVE CUTTER for matching, and one to the SOUND MIXER to use in the MIX.

SCREEN
The surface onto which films are PROJECTED. Usually made of opaque reflective material, the screen is perforated to allow sound to pass through. REAR PROJECTION screens are translucent.

SCREEN ACTORS GUILD *(Abbr. SAG)*
The actors' UNION which sets standards for wages, working conditions, etc.

SCREEN EXTRAS GUILD *(Abbr. SEG)*
Although not as strong or powerful as SAG or AFTRA, SEG performs the same functions for extras as the other unions do for their members.

SCREENING
A private showing of a film, or portions thereof, for a selected audience *(e.g., friends of the filmmakers, ACADEMY members, DISTRI-BUTORS).* No admission is charged.

SCREENING ROOM
A small theater equipped with a PROJECTION BOOTH for showing films, or films in the works. Every MAJOR STUDIO, LAB, OPTICAL HOUSE, etc., has several screening rooms. DAILIES are usually screened in a screening room unless circumstances (or preference) call for them to be looked at on an EDITING MACHINE.

SCREENPLAY *(aka SCRIPT, SCENARIO)*
The completed manuscript with DIALOGUE and often some camera directions, divided into SCENES, and written in the generally accepted screenplay form, upon which a film is based. Changes throughout PRODUCTION are not uncommon. *See also TELEPLAY.*

SCREENPLAY BY
The CREDIT awarded the WRITER (or writers) of a screenplay. This credit differs for WRITTEN BY in that it implies that the original story was not conceived by the writer. WRITTEN BY implies story and screenplay by the writer (or writers).

SCREEN TEST
An AUDITION recorded on film or tape to see if an actor is right for a part, or to see how someone looks on film.

SCREENWRITER
The person(s) who writes film SCRIPTS (SCREENPLAYS), TREATMENTS, story outlines, etc., for motion pictures and television.

SCREEN WRITERS GUILD
See WGA.

SCRIM
A translucent screen made of wire gauze, placed in front of a light source to diffuse the intensity of the light.

SCRIPT
See SCREENPLAY.

SCRIPT BREAKDOWN
See BREAKDOWN.

SCRIPT SUPERVISOR *(aka CONTINUITY CLERK)*
A member of the CREW who records detailed notes on every TAKE, including DIALOGUE, gestures, action, LENS used, costumes, make-up, etc., so as to ensure CONTINUITY of all of these elements from SHOT to shot and SCENE to scene. Films are usually shot out of sequence, so these notes are vastly important to the continuity of the finished product. These notes are submitted at the end of each shooting day, and are an essential tool for the EDITOR and DIRECTOR when putting the film together. Some feel that the script supervisor is the second most important job on the SET after the director. Without the help of this person, the director's job would be infinitely more difficult, as there are so many details to keep track of while shooting a film.

SECONDARY LOCATIONS
As with PRINCIPAL PLAYERS and SUPPORTING PLAYERS, there are locations that are deemed more important (PRIMARY LOCATIONS) and those that are less important (secondary locations). When scouting locations, it is advisable to find the primary locations, then find secondary locations nearby.

SECOND ASSISTANT CAMERAMAN
A member of the Camera Department who reports to the FIRST ASSISTANT CAMERAMAN and prepares the camera equipment for the First Assistant Cameraman. He loads and unloads magazines from the camera, fills out the CAMERA REPORTS, slaps the CLAP - STICKS at the beginning or end of each take.

SECOND ASSISTANT DIRECTOR
A production position who reports to the FIRST ASSISTANT DIRECTOR and the PRODUCTION MANAGER, and is generally responsible for all CAST and CREW. Duties include: to prepare and distribute daily paperwork (CALL SHEETS, PRODUCTION REPORTS, ACTOR'S TIME SHEETS, EXTRA'S VOUCHERS, etc.), and to maintain a liaison between the production manger and/or the production office and the First Assistant Director; to assist the First AD in the placement of Extras and in the maintenance of crowd control; and to supervise and direct the work of any DGA TRAINEE assigned to the project. On UNION productions, the Second is a member of the

DGA or some equivalent union covering production personnel *(e.g., Directors Guild of Canada, Directors Guild of Great Britain).* Can be UP-GRADED on SECOND UNIT to First AD. *See also KEY SECOND, SECOND SECOND.*

SECOND CAMERA
An additional camera used to shoot SEQUENCES at the same time as the principal camera. A second camera is generally used in SCENES that are difficult to re-stage, such as a building collapsing or a gas station blowing up. *See also MULTIPLE CAMERAS.*

SECOND CAMERAMAN
See CAMERA OPERATOR.

SECOND FEATURE *(aka B PICTURE)*
The lesser draw in a DOUBLE FEATURE.

SECOND SECOND
On a production requiring more than one SECOND ASSISTANT DIRECTOR, these are the additional Second Assistant Directors who are hired and who report to the KEY SECOND ASSISTANT DIRECTOR. They are usually hired on a day-to-day basis and are called upon to help with a large cast or extra CALL, or in large crowd scenes. However, there are exceptions: On *TAXI DRIVER* , due to the complexity of the show (a great deal of the shooting was done at night on the streets in New York), an additional Second Assistant Director (Bill Eustace) was hired for the entire schedule.

SECOND UNIT
An additional PRODUCTION CREW used for shooting SEQUENCES that do not involve PRINCIPAL PLAYERS, such as BACKGROUND shots at remote LOCATIONS, backgrounds for PROCESS SHOTS, large-scale sequences shot with multiple cameras, and INSERTS. This crew is handled by the SECOND UNIT DIRECTOR. Often the SECOND AD becomes the FIRST AD of the second unit, and on non-union productions, the CAMERA OPERATOR may become the second unit DIRECTOR OF PHOTOGRAPHY.

SECOND UNIT DIRECTOR
The person in charge of directing SEQUENCES not involving PRINCIPAL PLAYERS. *See SECOND UNIT, INSERT.*

SECOND UNIT DIRECTOR OF PHOTOGRAPHY
A cameraman hired to shoot SCENES that fall into the second unit category. Shots that the principal unit does not have time to shoot,

shots that are very complicated or require special skills or equipment *(e.g., underwater scenes)*, or shots that are at a distant LOCATION, or INSERTS, are all instances of situations in which a second unit DP could be hired. The first unit CAMERA OPERATOR and ASSISTANT CAMERAMAN can be UP-GRADED for second unit to do the necessary shots.

SEG
Abbreviation for SCREEN EXTRAS GUILD.

SEGUE
Pronounced *"seg-way,"* the term comes from radio and early television days and means to move from one SCENE to the next, usually accompanied by a short piece of music (BRIDGE).

SELSYN MOTOR
A trade name for a device that runs two pieces of equipment in SYNCHRONIZATION *(e.g., camera and sound recorder.)*

SENIOR
A heavy-duty spotlight for 5000-watts.

SENSURROUND
A trademark for a sound system developed by Universal Studios that adds low-frequency vibrations to the SOUND TRACK, increasing the believability of the action in such films as EARTHQUAKE.

SEPARATION NEGATIVES
Three individual negatives, each sensitive to one of the PRIMARY COLORS of light, used in THREE-STRIPE TECHNICOLOR. These three negatives are bonded together to produce an INTEGRAL TRIPACK.

SEQUENCE
A series of SHOTS with a CONTINUITY of LOCATION, ACTION, time, or story and usually with a beginning, middle and end.

SERIES
A weekly or daily program on television, usually one half hour or one hour in length. *See also PILOT.*

SET
The exterior or interior LOCATION where a film or television show is shot. The person responsible for the look of a set is the PRODUCTION DESIGNER or ART DIRECTOR.

SET DECORATOR
The person responsible for DRESSING the SET with furnishings
relevant to the various scenes.

SET DESIGNER
The person responsible for planning the construction of the SETS,
from the description and drawings of the ART DIRECTOR/
PRODUCTION DESIGNER.

SET DRESSING
Furnishings, etc. that will be used to decorate the set. *See also PROP.*

SET ESTIMATOR
A member of the ART DEPARTMENT responsible for preparing Cost
Estimates for the construction of the sets, based upon detailed drawings,
or sometimes just verbal descriptions of the desired set.

SET-UP
The arrangement of the camera, lights, equipment, actors, etc., in their
correct positions before shooting.

SFX
Common abbreviation for SOUND EFFECTS.

SHARED CARD
Two or more names appearing at the same time on the SCREEN in the
CREDITS.

SHARP
A crisp IMAGE in proper FOCUS.

SHOOT (n.)
Slang for the filming of a motion picture or television show, etc. *(e.g.,
"How did the shoot go today?" or "This shoot is driving me nuts!")*

SHOOT (v.)
To film any part, or all, of a motion picture or television show, etc.
(e.g., "Get ready to shoot this before we lose the light.")

SHOOTING COMPANY
The CREW on a film.

SHOOTING RATIO
The ratio of the amount of film EXPOSED while shooting to the amount of film in the final RELEASE PRINT. A 4:1 ratio is considered economical. A 20:1 ratio is considered wasteful. Luis Buñuel was reknown for shooting 1:1.

SHOOTING SCHEDULE
A detailed list of everyone and everything needed to shoot every SCENE in a SCRIPT, and when each is to be shot. It is compiled from the information on the BREAKDOWN SHEETS and PRODUCTION BOARD.

SHOOTING SCRIPT
Approved final version of the SCREENPLAY with full DIALOGUE, detailed camera SET-UPS and other instructions used by the DIRECTOR.

SHORT SUBJECT *(aka SHORT)*
A film that runs 30 minutes or less.

SHORT END
A length of unexposed film that is left after cutting off the exposed part. Many student and experimental films are made from short ends.

SHOT
One continuous TAKE. *See also SCENE, SEQUENCE.*

SHOTGUN MIKE
A directional microphone that can pick up sound from a limited area. The angle of acceptance is more limited than that of a DIRECTIONAL MIKE. A shotgun mike is to a directional mike what a TELEPHOTO LENS is to a normal lens.

SHOW CARDS
See CUE CARDS.

SHRINKAGE
The reduction in film size due to loss of moisture during PROCESSING or to extended storage. The resulting IMAGE may be distorted and the film will have a tendency to tear because of stress during PROJECTION.

SHUTTER
An automatic device in a camera designed to allow light to expose the film while the individual FRAME is in position, and to obstruct light when the film is being moved into position.

SIDE CAR MOUNT
A special attachment that holds the camera onto the side of a vehicle for filming. *See CAMERA MOUNT, CAR MOUNT.*

SIGNATORY
A company that has signed an agreement with a UNION or GUILD obligating them to comply with the rules and regulations of that union or guild.

SILENT *(aka SILENT BIT)*
An actor who has no lines to deliver, but who contributes to the ACTION of a SCENE. For example, the waiter who spills hot soup on the principal actor is a silent bit. The other waiters who wait on the tables are considered EXTRAS.

SILENT PRINT *(aka PICTURE PRINT)*
Processed film with a positive IMAGE and no SOUND TRACK.

SILENT SPEED
For film not intended to be used with sound, the proper rate is 16-18 FPS.

SILHOUETTE
A backlit subject whose front shows little or no detail to the camera other than its general outline.

SILK *(aka BUTTERFLY)*
A large, rectangular cloth used to DIFFUSE harsh light during shooting. It is mainly used outdoors.

SINGLE BROAD
See BROAD.

SINGLE CARD
A CREDIT where only one name appears on the SCREEN. This is more desirable than a SHARED CARD, and if not agreed upon during contract negotiations, may be considered a DEAL BREAKER.

SINGLE FRAME EXPOSURE
A technique used in ANIMATION, Stop Motion and Time Lapse photography in which film is exposed frame by frame.

SINGLES
When shooting COVERAGE of a SCENE, the DIRECTOR usually shoots some CLOSE-UPS of individual actors in the scene saying their key lines and/or listening (a REACTION SHOT). These shots of a single person are called singles. A single can be any sort of a shot: close-up, MEDIUM SHOT, etc., as long as there is only one person in the shot.

SINGLE SYSTEM
A method of recording sound and picture onto the same piece of film. Its use today is generally limited to news and some DOCUMENTARY work, as the quality is not as good as DOUBLE SYSTEM (separate picture and sound) and it presents problems (limitations) when EDITING.

SKIP FRAMING
An OPTICAL PRINTING technique used to speed up action, in which every other, or every third FRAME is printed. DOUBLE PRINTING is the opposite of skip framing, and is used to slow down action by printing frames two or three times.

SKY FILTER
A graduated filter that darkens only the sky when shooting in black and white.

SLATE *(aka CLAPSTICKS, CLAPPERBOARD)*
Hinged boards which, when clapped, provide a CUE for SYNCHRON-IZATION of sound and picture during EDITING. Information is written on the slate to identify each TAKE: film's title, name of DIRECTOR, CINEMATOGRAPHER, ROLL number, SCENE NUMBER, take number and date. The call for ACTION does not come until after the slate.

SLEEPER
A film that becomes a BOXOFFICE HIT to (most) everyone's surprise.

SLOP PRINT
See SCRATCH PRINT.

SLOW MOTION
An effect achieved by running the film through the camera at speeds greater than 24 FPS, or through the projector at slower-than-normal speed (rarely done). The opposite is ACCELERATED MOTION.

SLUG
A piece of LEADER or otherwise unusable film that is temporarily inserted in a WORK PRINT to replace damaged, unfinished or missing FOOTAGE. *See also FILL.*

SMOKE/FOG EFFECTS
Machine-generated, realistic and quickly produced effects used to simulate smoke or fog, indoors or out. They are safe, long-lasting and have no unpleasant odor.

SMPTE
Abbreviation for SOCIETY OF MOTION PICTURE AND TELE-VISION ENGINEERS.

SNEAK PREVIEW
An advance showing of a film in a theater to a paying audience to test reaction, or to generate word-of-mouth in the community. Changes are often made after a picture is sneaked.

SNOOT
A cone-like attachment that fits on the front of a light source used to direct light to a certain area of the SET.

SNOW EFFECT
Used for SCENES where snow is desired, made of shredded plastic or feathers.

SOCIETY OF MOTION PICTURE AND TELEVISION ENGINEERS *(Abbr. SMPTE)*
A professional organization that sets technical standards for the motion picture and television industry. *See also UNIVERSAL LEADER.*

SOFT FOCUS
A term used when the FOCUS PULLER or technician did not focus the LENS properly, causing the resulting IMAGE to be fuzzy or unclear. This is not to be confused with the process of shooting with a DIFFUSION FILTER or gauze (or vaseline) in front of the lens, to create an intentionally romantic or hazy effect. *See DIFFUSED LIGHT.*

SOFT LIGHT
A light source that, through the use of DIFFUSERS or GELS, casts a gentle glow on a SET, with a minimum of shadows. This is also the name of a particular lamp (bulb).

SOFT WIPE
A WIPE whose edges are blurred.

SOUND
The audio portion of a film that is recorded on MAGNETIC TAPE or MAGNETIC FILM. Several separate TRACKS (MUSIC, EFFECTS, DIALOGUE) can be recorded and MIXED later to create the COMPOSITE SOUND TRACK. A recent invention is DOLBY, a noise-reducing system, that has greatly improved the fidelity of motion picture sound.

SOUND CAMERA
A specially designed, BLIMPED camera whose mechanical noise is sufficiently diminished so as not to be picked up by the mike during shooting. *See BARNEY, SOUND.*

SOUND CREW
Usually a three-person crew consisting of PRODUCTION MIXER/SOUNDMAN/RECORDIST (not to be confused with POST PRODUCTION MIXER who mixes all the TRACKS when the picture is cut), the BOOM OPERATOR, and the CABLE PULLER.

SOUND EFFECTS *(Abbr. SFX)*
The third part of a SOUND TRACK in which all artificially created or natural sounds other than MUSIC or DIALOGUE are recorded. Sounds, such as a door opening, a bird chirping, glass breaking, are recorded separately (WILD SOUND) or transferred from a LIBRARY of sound effects. *See also FOLEY.*

SOUND SPEED
The standard rate at which film or tape passes through the camera when it is being shot IN SYNC with sound.

SOUND STAGE
A large, soundproof building, usually on a STUDIO LOT, where, in general, interior SCENES for films are shot.

SOUND STRIPE
A thin strip of ferromagnetic coating applied to the film's edge on which the SOUND TRACK is placed.

SOUND TRACK
1) The audio portion of a film that is divided into three or four separate tracks or channels - DIALOGUE, MUSIC, EFFECTS and a spillover track for additional effects. An OPTICAL SOUND TRACK is made from the MIXED tracks, then is printed onto the side of the film in the LAB. It is not uncommon for many separate units (there can be hundreds) to be individually EDITED and then be MIXED to produce the final sound track. 2) Another term for the recorded version of a film's musical SCORE, available on albums, tapes and compact disks.

SOUP
Slang for the chemicals (DEVELOPER) in which film is DEVELOPED.

SPAGHETTI WESTERN
Nickname given to genre of film popular in the 60s. They were Westerns made in Italy, usually on low BUDGETS. This is where Clint Eastwood and DIRECTOR Sergio Leone (the most famous of the spaghetti Western directors) got their starts.

SPECIAL CAMERA OPERATOR
A member of the CAMERA CREW who specializes in a particular kind of CINEMATOGRAPHY, such as underwater, HAND-HELD, aerial, etc. These operators are usually hired on a daily basis depending upon the complexity and duration of the job.

SPECIAL EFFECTS *(Abbr. SP-FX)*
Any effect that is special, extraordinary, and must be created. This can range from a PRACTICAL (working) sink and garbage disposal to the most intricate EFFECTS as seen in STAR WARS, ET, etc. All the elements - fire, air and water in all their various forms (rain, mud, hurricanes, floods, fires, etc) and their resulting damage (exploding buildings, mountain cave-ins, avalanches, etc.) are all the responsibility of the SPECIAL EFFECTS DEPARTMENT. *See also BLUE SCREEN PROJECTION, CHROMA KEY, MATTE SHOT, MINIATURE.*

SPECIAL EFFECTS DEPARTMENT
That division of the PRODUCTION CREW (or sometimes an independent company) that is in charge of producing all the special

effects on a PRODUCTION, from the elaborate (STAR WARS) to the very simple (a working sink).

SPECIAL PORTABLE CAMERA
Special HAND-HELD cameras that mount on BODY FRAMES to allow fluid photography while moving. Two brand names are Panaglide and STEADICAM. They are used for SCENES that would be impossible to shoot with a standard camera on a TRIPOD or DOLLY.

SPEED (n.)
1) The rate that film travels through the CAMERA, PROJECTOR or PRINTER, usually expressed in FRAMES PER SECOND (FPS), or in feet per minute. The normal speeds are 24 fps, or 90 feet per minute for 35mm film. *See also FOOTAGE.*   2) A film's sensitivity to light as expressed in ASA, DIN or ISO numbers.

SPEED! (v.)
The CUE to the DIRECTOR from the SOUNDMAN (PRODUCTION MIXER) that the sound recorder is running at the proper speed for recording in SYNCHRONIZATION with the picture.

SP-FX
Abbreviation for SPECIAL EFFECTS.

SPIDER
A special metal device that helps steady a camera on a TRIPOD in slippery situations.

SPIDER BOX
Film industry term for junction box - an electrical unit with outlets for a number of lighting units.

SPILL LIGHT
Excessive and unwanted light falling on a subject or on a SET where it should not be.

SPLICE
The joining of two pieces of film. The two types of splice are the HOT (or CEMENT) SPLICE, in which scraped ends of film are cemented together, and the DRY or TAPE SPLICE, in which the ends of film are joined together and taped without overlapping.

SPLICER
The device used to join ends of film. Three types of splicers are: HOT SPLICER, used for cement splices, HAND SPLICER, a tape splicer

operated by hand, MACHINE SPLICER *(aka GRISWOLD)*, a hot splicer operated by hands and feet.

SPLIT FOCUS
A technique for keeping two objects, one in the BACKGROUND and one in the FOREGROUND, in focus by focusing on a point in between.

SPLIT REEL
A reel whose flanges screw together (and unscrew) so that film on CORES (instead of reels) can be wound and rewound.

SPLIT SCREEN
A SPECIAL EFFECTS shot where two or more separate IMAGES are composited in the same FRAME, thus are seen on the screen at the same time *(e.g., Rock Hudson and Doris Day talking to each other on the phone in PILLOW TALK. We see him on his phone on one side of the screen, and her on her phone on the other).*   Used more in the 60s and early 70s, this effect is achieved by MASKING one part of the frame and EXPOSING the other, then reversing the process. Due to time and cost considerations, this is usually done OPTICALLY.

SPOTLIGHT *(aka SPOT)*
A focusable lamp. Most of the lights on a SET are spotlights.

SPOTTING SESSION
A time during POST PRODUCTION when the DIRECTOR, COMPOSER, EDITOR and MUSIC EDITOR determine where the music (SCORE) for a film should fall.

SPROCKET HOLE
See PERFORATIONS, PITCH.

SPROCKETS
Small gears in the CAMERA, PROJECTOR or PRINTER that advances the film. *See PERFORATIONS.*

SPUN
Short for spun glass. Today, spun, which is used as a light DIFFUSER, is made out of synthetic material instead of actual spun glass, which can hurt people's hands or lungs.

SQUEEZE LENS
An industry term for ANAMORPHIC LENS.

SQUIB
An electrically-ignited device that causes pre-programmed targets to appear to have been hit by bullets. The ends of two wires are dipped into a pyrotechnic composition. When voltage is applied, the wires short out, causing a flash. When a squib is used on a person (to make it appear that he/she has been shot), a backing is put on the squib so the explosion can only go foreward, so as not to injure the actor. A small packet of blood is built into the squib so that area will ooze blood when the person is *hit*. This is called a Bullet Effect.

STAGE
1) The raised platform in a theater upon which a play is performed.
2) An indoor or outdoor area on which SETS are constructed and filming takes place. *See also SOUND STAGE.*

STANDARD SCRIPT FORMAT
The preferred form in which SCREENPLAYS are typed or written. If other formats are used, it can affect a PRODUCTION MANAGER'S calculations in judging how long it will take to shoot the piece.

STANDARD STOCK
Thirty-five millimeter film.

STAND-IN
A person who takes the place of the STAR while a SCENE is being SET UP and lit.

STANDING SET
A permanent outdoor or indoor set.

STAR
A well-known actor or actress in a leading or CAMEO role. Oftentimes, a project can be financed solely on the acceptance by a star to play a role.

STARTED
Usually refers to the first day an actor works. As there are many rules governing an actor once he/she begins work, the proper start date is very important. *See DROP AND PICK UP, RUN OF SHOW.*

START MARK
A CUE mark on the film LEADER and its SOUND TRACK to denote the SYNCHRONIZATION point. Start marks are also used on COMPOSITE PRINTS to assist the PROJECTIONIST in readying the film for projection. *See also CHANGEOVERS.*

STATIC MARKS
Dark streaks on film due to friction in the camera, or improper handling, often occurring in cold weather.

STATION 12
A department of the SCREEN ACTORS GUILD which confirms that an actor is an active member in good standing of SAG and that all dues have been paid in full.

STEADICAM
Trade name for a BODY FRAME that assists in steadying a hand-held camera. In 1977 a special ACADEMY AWARD for scientific and technical achievement was presented to its developers. PANAVISION developed a similar device called PANAGLIDE.

STEENBECK
Brand name of a FLATBED EDITING machine used for editing and viewing film. *See also KEM.*

STEP DEAL
A development arrangement whereby the decision to proceed is made after approval or completion of certain steps *(e.g., SYNOPSIS, TREATMENT, FIRST DRAFT, FINAL SCREENPLAY.)*

STEP OUTLINE
See SYNOPSIS.

STEP PRINTING
An OPTICAL printing process in which the film is held with REGISTRATION PINS and is printed FRAME by frame to insure maximum steadiness. This is used for projected BACKGROUNDS, TRAVELLING MATTES, etc., when steadiness is an important factor.

STEREOPHONIC SOUND
An audio reproduction method used since the 50s in most WIDE SCREEN productions. Today many standard format films are RELEASED in stereo. It add fullness and realism and gives a feeling of movement by recording sound through separate MIKES onto separate TRACKS, which are then PLAYED BACK through separate speakers corresponding to the placement of the mikes. Stereophonic sound quality is especially important for music and SOUND EFFECTS.

STEREOSCOPIC CINEMA *(aka 3-D)*
A technique of projecting a film in such a way as an illusion of three dimensional vision is achieved, using special 3-D viewing glasses. Several different patented processes are used today.

STILL
1) A photograph shot with a still, not a motion picture, camera. 2) An 8x10 inch glossy black and white or color photograph of an actor or SCENE from a film usually used for PUBLICITY purposes. *See HEAD SHOT.*

STILL PHOTOGRAPHER
The person responsible for taking STILLS on a movie SET, to be used for matching/CONTINUITY in later SHOTS *(e.g. hair, COSTUMES, make-up, SET DECORATION)*, or later on, for PUBLICITY purposes.

STOCK *(aka RAWSTOCK)*
Negative film that has not been EXPOSED.

STOCK FOOTAGE *(aka LIBRARY FOOTAGE)*
Film footage from different eras, different places, of different things that can be duplicated and incorporated into a new PRODUCTION. Used when certain shots would be too costly, difficult or simply impossible to recreate. Stock footage can be of ships sinking, cars on highways in certain locales, aerial views, Times Square in 1945, etc. You can usually tell when old stock footage has been used, due to the difference in old and new film STOCK, and the fact that the stock footage (which has been DUPED then inserted into the film) has an extra GENERATION and, thus, is GRAINIER.

STOP
See APERTURE, F-STOP, T-NUMBER.

STOP DOWN
To reduce the size of the LENS APERTURE, in order to reduce the amount of light and increase the DEPTH OF FIELD by adjusting the DIAPHRAGM. *See also ASTIGMATISM.*

STOP FRAME
See FREEZE FRAME, HOLD FRAME.

STOP MOTION
A technique used in ANIMATION, in which the object to be animated is moved after the EXPOSURE of each FRAME or two. Also widely

used in shooting television commercials where inanimate objects appear to move.

STORY ANALYST
A member of the story department who reads and analyzes literary material (SCREENPLAYS, TREATMENTS, magazine articles, books, etc.) that is submitted each week to the Story Department. The resulting synopses prepared by the Story Analyst are called COVERAGE, and are submitted to the STORY EDITOR for review. *See READER.*

STORYBOARD
1) A series of drawings or photographs that show the progression of SHOTS in a film SEQUENCE (generally an action sequence that is expensive to shoot) or for an entire film. Alfred Hitchcock was famous for never beginning to shoot his films without having complete storyboards showing each shot in detail. 2) Storyboards are used extensively in the production of commercials. They are created by the advertising agency for sponsor approval, then are distributed to PRODUCTION COMPANIES for bids.

STORY EDITOR
A member of a STUDIO'S story department and supervisor of several STORY ANALYSTS. The job entails reviewing the COVERAGE submitted by the analysts, then passing them on to the Production VP's with recommendations as to whether or not the property should be acquired and/or DEVELOPED.

STRAIGHT CUT
A cut from one SHOT directly to another, with no OPTICAL EFFECTS.

STREAMER
An EDITING mark used as an indication to the OPTICAL HOUSE, RE-RECORDING MIXER and FOLEY ARTIST where FADES, DISSOLVES EFFECTS, TITLES and other POST PRODUCTION effects are to go.

STRESS MARKS
Streaks that occur on a film PRINT due to pressure or friction on the NEGATIVE. *See also ABRASIONS.*

STRIKE
1) To tear down a SET when shooting has been completed. It is advisable not to strike any set until the DAILIES have been approved.

2) To refuse to work due to a labor GRIEVANCE. 3) To create a print from a NEGATIVE *(i.e., to strike a print).*

STRIPE
A band of magnetic coating that is applied to film. In making a magnetic COMPOSITE PRINT, the final SOUND TRACK is TRANSFERRED onto these magnetic stripes.

STROBE
A rapidly flashing light that causes the subject being photographed (in motion pictures) to appear to move in a jerky, disjointed manner. This effect is usually caused by an uneven relationship between the speed of the object being filmed and the intervals between EXPOSURES.

STUDIO (LOT)
1) (LOT) Physical location and facilities (offices, SOUND STAGES, etc.) existing for use by either in-house or independent PRODUCTION COMPANIES for DEVELOP-MENT, PRODUCTION and POST PRODUCTION of motion pictures and television shows. 2) A film shot *in a studio* means shot in specially built SETS on sound stages or studio back lots *(e.g., NEW YORK, NEW YORK, which was shot primarily on sound stages and back lots in Los Angeles),* as opposed to being shot on LOCATION *(e.g., MEAN STREETS, shot on locations in New York.)*

STUDIO (MAJOR)
An organization that DEVELOPS, PRODUCES and DISTRIBUTES motion pictures and television shows. In the old days of Hollywood, the studios were much more powerful and self sufficient than their modern day counterparts. They kept their own stable of PRODUCERS, DIRECTORS, ACTORS and WRITERS under contract, as well as having ongoing ART, COSTUME, MAKE-UP, PUBLICITY, etc. DEPARTMENTS. They had everything necessary for every phase of making movies, from concept to completion, to DISTRIBUTION and EXPLOITATION and even EXHI-BITION. These days, studios hire as needed for the most part, instead of keeping large numbers of people on staff full time. There are some departments, however, *(e.g., legal, STORY, advertising, DISTRIBUTION, etc.)* which are maintained on an ongoing basis. Recent legal developments may allow studios to return to exhibition.

STUDIO ZONE
Many major cities have specified areas, of a certain radius from a central point. In Los Angeles, it is a radius of 30 miles from the old AMPTP headquarters at La Cienega and Fairfax. Anything outside that area is

considered to be a DISTANT LOCATION. More precisely, any location where the CAST and CREW are required to spend the night is considered a distant location, and anything else is considered to be within the studio zone. If the location is a long drive, but not far enough away to necessitate spending the night (LOCAL LOCATION), then employees are compensated for MILEAGE.

STUNT *(aka GAG)*
A dangerous, or potentially dangerous, act or action performed by an actor or a specially trained STUNT PERSON/S.

STUNT ADJUSTMENT
The premium paid in addition to the GUILD (SAG or AFTRA) DAY RATE to the STUNTMAN/WOMAN by the PRODUCTION COMPANY. The amount is commensurate to the complexity, relative danger or level of expertise required.

STUNT COORDINATOR
A member of the CREW responsible for the organization and coordination of all stunts on a PRODUCTION.

STUNT DOUBLE *(aka STUNTMAN, STUNTWOMAN, STUNT PHOTO DOUBLE)*
A stunt person who closely resembles (or is made to resemble) an actor in a film, and takes his or her place in dangerous or potentially dangerous scenes.

SUBJECTIVE CAMERA
See POINT OF VIEW.

SUBMERGED PRINTING
See LIQUID GATE.

SUBTITLES
The lines of translated DIALOGUE that appear at the bottom of the SCREEN over the IMAGE in a foreign language film (when the dialogue has not been DUBBED).

SUBTRACTIVE PROCESS
A method used in color photography to achieve color by FILTERING out other colors from white light. *See PRIMARY COLORS, ADDITIVE PROCESS.*

SUNGUN
A portable, battery-powered, high intensity light, used mostly for news or DOCUMENTARY work.

SUNLIGHT
Light directly from the sun as opposed to DAYLIGHT that includes skylight and REFLECTED sunlight.

SUNSHADE
See MATTE BOX.

SUPERIMPOSITION
Photographing or PRINTING one or more IMAGES over each other so they can all be seen at once. This effect can be achieved through multiple EXPOSURES (in the camera) of the same piece of film, or by OPTICALLY printing several images onto one piece of film.

SUPPORTING PLAYERS
The second leads in a film or TV show.

SWASHBUCKLER
A dashing, flamboyant rogue, like Errol Flynn, John Barrymore and, more recently, Harrison Ford in *STAR WARS* and the *INDIANA JONES* films. The swashbuckler film is an action/adventure film loaded with good humor and fun. There is always a dashing hero who saves the day for someone, usually a beautiful maiden in some sort of distress. Peter O'Toole portrayed an aging swashbuckler in *MY FAVORITE YEAR*.

SWEETEN
To make small improvements in a SOUND TRACK.

SWING GANG
The people working under the SET DECORATOR and LEAD MAN who DRESS and STRIKE the SET. They always precede and then follow the shooting company.

SWISH PAN *(aka WHIP PAN, ZIP PAN)*
A rapid movement of the camera from right to left (or vice versa) causing a blurred IMAGE. It is mainly used for dramatic effect.

SYNC
Abbreviation for SYNCHRONIZATION.

SYNCHRONIZATION
When the picture and its sound coincide properly, the film is IN SYNC. Any other situation is considered OUT OF SYNC.

SYNCHRONIZER
An EDITING device with interlocking sprocketed wheels that allows the EDITOR (or assistant) to keep the sound and picture IN SYNC.

SYNCHRONOUS SOUND
1) Sound in a motion picture that directly corresponds to the IMAGE *(e.g., screeching brakes heard when we see a foot slamming down on the brake pedal).* ASYNCHRONOUS SOUND might show the face of a woman looking on in horror as she hears the sound of the screeching brakes.　2) Sound recorded in SYNCRONIZATION with the film being shot in the camera.

SYNC MARK
See START MARK.

SYNC PULSE
A 60-cycle pulse used to keep sound and picture IN SYNC.

SYNOPSIS
Usually a short, written outline of the story line of a proposed motion picture. In STEP DEALS, usually a synopsis is presented, then a TREATMENT, and finally a SCREENPLAY.

T

TACHOMETER
A device on the motion picture camera that shows the speed at which it is running. It is read by the ASSISTANT CAMERAMAN to make sure the camera is running at the correct speed.

TAFT-HARTLEY
A labor law that permits anyone to accept a job and continue working for thirty days before being required to join any UNION or GUILD that might be affected.

TAG
A short SCENE, almost like an afterthought, at the end of a television show or film.

TAIL
The end of a roll of film.

TAILS OUT
When film is wound backwards on the REEL or roll with the end of the reel (tail) at the beginning. Prints that are tails out must be rewound before being PROJECTED, as the first FRAMES coming off the reel are the last frames of the picture.

TAKE
A single, continuous SHOT made by the camera. There may be several takes of each shot, until the DIRECTOR gets what he/she wants from both the actors and the technical crew. Luis Buñuel was reknown for shooting only one take of each shot on many of his films.

TAKE A MEETING
Trendy Hollywood slang meaning to have a meeting.

TAKE-UP REEL
The reel that collects the viewed or PROJECTED film. *See TAILS OUT.*

TALENT
On-camera and off-camera performers, including animals.

TAPE
See MAGNETIC TAPE.

TAPE SPLICE
See SPLICE.

TARGET
A round screen that blocks light from wherever it is not wanted. *See GOBO, FLAG.*

TEACHER
See WELFARE WORKER.

TECHNICAL ADVISOR
An expert consultant on a motion picture or television show who ensures that details in his/her specialized area are authentic. For example, a retired airline pilot may be asked to offer advice on the workings of a 747, or a native of Bali to verify details in the SCRIPT *(e.g., COSTUMES, DIALOGUE, MAKE-UP).*

TECHNICAL COORDINATOR
The person responsible for assisting the director on a multi-camera project (scene, episode, feature film, etc.) photographed continuously either before a live audience or as if there were one present. The Coordinator's chief responsibility is to supervise the movement of each camera throughtout the show.

TECHNICOLOR
A trademarked color process invented during World War I by Herbert T. Kalmus and Daniel F. Comstock. Originally, it was a process that combined two colors (red and green) on the screen by means for a special PROJECTOR. This process, however, was very expensive and produced unsatisfactory color.

In 1932, a new, more accurate and eye-pleasing Technicolor was developed: THREE STRIPE, using three NEGATIVES individually sensitive to the PRIMARY COLORS (red, green and blue) and printed onto a single strand of film in the LAB. *See also INTEGRAL TRIPACK.*

TELECINE
The process by which film is TRANSFERRED to tape. *See also KINESCOPE, RANK CINTEL.*

TELEPHOTO LENS
A lens with a FOCAL LENGTH longer than that of a normal lens. Its main ability is to photograph distant subjects as if they were close up. The telephoto, however, decreases the DEPTH OF FIELD. *See also LONG FOCUS LENS, ZOOM LENS.*

TELEPROMPTER
An electronic CUING device that replaces handwritten CUE CARDS. There are two kinds: a MONITOR mounted near the camera LENS, and a mirror housing that fits over the lens so the actor (or news broadcaster) can look into the lens and see the lines to be read.

TEMPO
The speed and rhythm of the progression of a film.

TENNER
A heavy-duty spotlight that uses a 10,000-watt lamp.

THEME
1) The basic idea of a film.   2) A musical passage identified with a person or place *(e.g., Lara's Theme in DR. ZHIVAGO).*

THIN NEGATIVE
An UNDEREXPOSED negative with little or no density.

35MM
The standard gauge of film and equipment used in professional motion picture making. 35mm film is 35 millimeters wide, has 16 FRAMES per foot, and 4 PERFORATIONS per frame.

THREAD
To place film over the SPROCKETS and through the GATE and paths of the camera, PROJECTOR or PRINTER.

3-D
Three-dimensional films, where the illusion of three-dimensions is created. *See STEREOSCOPIC.*

THREE-STRIP
The original TECHNICOLOR process.

THROW
The distance between the IMAGE on the screen and the LENS of the PROJECTOR.

TIGHT SHOT
A shot in which the subject is the only IMAGE on the screen. It literally means to be framed tightly around the subject. *See also CLOSE-UP.*

TILT
The up and down movement of a camera as opposed to the sideways movement used in a PAN.

TIME LAPSE
A method of EXPOSING FRAMES of film at a single time, or at pre-set intervals. When the film is PROJECTED at normal speed, it appears that the action has been sped up *(e.g., small plants emerging from the ground, a spider spinning its web, the movie KOYAANISQATSI).*

TIMER
The LABORATORY technician who evaluates the COLOR BALANCE of each SHOT and orders any necessary COLOR CORRECTIONS.

TIMING
1) An actor's ability to create the proper TEMPO in a SCENE through the rhythm and flow of his or her PERFORMANCE. 2) A LAB technician's evaluation of the density and COLOR BALANCE of each SHOT of the film, so as to achieve the desired contrast and color balance. 3) Referring to the actual running time of a proposed motion picture, the SCRIPT timing is usually performed by the SCRIPT SUPERVISOR. It is a detailed analysis of exactly how long (to the second) each SCENE will run. Having a script timed early on in the

preparation of a project can save the PRODUCER a great deal of money. Scenes that appear to be too long can be cut down in the writing instead of waiting until the EDITING ROOM.

TITLES
The printed words at the beginning and end of a film. The name of the film at the beginning is referred to as the MAIN TITLE. The others are referred to simply as FRONT CREDITS. Titles SUPERIMPOSED on the bottom of the FRAME (usually for translation purposes) are known as SUBTITLES.

T-NUMBER
See T-STOP.

TONAL KEY
The range of light and dark tones in an IMAGE. HIGH KEY signifies a bright SCENE with mainly light tones, and no heavy shadows. LOW KEY signifies a scene with heavy shadows and few light tones.

TONING
A chemical process that turns black and white film to sepia.

TOP BILLING
The CREDIT(s) placed in the most advantageous position vis-a-vis the MAIN TITLE of the picture on the SCREEN, and in the paid advertising for the picture *(i.e., above the title and centered if there is one name, or above the title and to the left if there are two names.)* In the event there are two STARS of equal stature, it is not unusual to see the credit on the right placed higher than the credit on the left so as to impart equal importance. Although top billing is usually something that DIRECTORS, PRODUCERS and ACTORS are more concerned with, it is not unusual to see CINEMA-TOGRAPHERS, EDITORS, COSTUME DESIGNERS and PRODUCTION DESIGNERS also negotiating for preferred billing.

TOP HAT
See HIGH HAT.

TOP SHEET
A summary sheet - the first page of a BUDGET form that provides the subtotals for each category listed in the budget, and the bottom line costs of a project.

TRACK (n.)
1) See SOUND TRACK.   2) Wooden or metal railing laid on the ground (or floor) on which the DOLLY moves smoothly for TRACKING SHOTS *(aka DOLLY SHOTS)*.

TRACK (v.)
To move the camera (on tracks) in order to follow the action in a SCENE.

TRACKING SHOT *(aka DOLLY SHOT, TRAVELING SHOT, TRUCKING SHOT)*
A moving shot where the camera follows the action in a SCENE. The camera is placed on a DOLLY that moves on TRACKS, or on a CAMERA CAR or other vehicle.

TRADES/TRADE PAPERS
Daily and weekly newspapers that specialize in the news of the entertainment business *(e.g., THE HOLLYWOOD REPORTER, VARIETY)*.

TRAILER
Usually a visual SYNOPSIS of a motion picture that has its own structure - not necessarily corresponding to that of the film. It is used to create an audience awareness of and interest in an upcoming RELEASE. Teaser trailers run less than ninety seconds and may be attached to the beginning of another FEATURE FILM released by the same STUDIO. Regular trailers may be of any length, but are usually less than two minutes. They are RATED by the MPAA *(see RATING)*. Today, TRAILERS are considered to be an art form in their own right, and reflect highly sophisticated aesthetic techniques combined with carefully determined marketing strategy.

TRAINEE, DGA
A person learning to become a SECOND ASSISTANT DIRECTOR in the DIRECTORS GUILD OF AMERICA. Very few applicants are accepted each year in the DGA Training Program. The trainee must pass a rigorous written and oral examination. Usually, there are more than 1500 candidates who apply each year for not more than two dozen places.

TRAINER
See HANDLER, WRANGLER.

TRANSFER
Any magnetic duplication, whether picture or sound *(e.g., to record a SOUND TRACK from the original one-quarter inch tape to magnetic film, or to record a film onto videotape)*. Going from one size video-tape to another is referred to as DUBBING.

TRANSITIONAL EFFECTS
See DISSOLVE, FADE, WIPE.

TRANSLITE
A backing that is lit to give the illusion of being outdoors.

TRANSPARENCY
An IMAGE on a transparent substance such as glass, film, etc., that is suitable for viewing or PROJECTING. STILL transparencies (slides) are often used in PROCESS SHOTS to project a BACKGROUND for a SCENE.

TRANSPORTATION
That department for the CREW responsible for transporting the crew and all necessary equipment and vehicles from the PRODUCTION. Cars used in front of the camera (called Picture Cars), however, are (sometimes) the responsibility of the PROP department.

TRAVEL
For LOCATION shooting, a travel day is considered work time. CAST and CREW are to be paid for travel time.

TRAVELING MATTE
A complex system used to combine two or more action SCENES shot at separate times in order to make them appear to be part of the same SHOT when they are PROJECTED.

TRAVELING SHOT
A shot in which the camera moves on a DOLLY, a CAMERA CAR or some other sort of vehicle. *See DOLLY SHOT, TRACKING SHOT.*

TREATMENT
A very detailed STORY OUTLINE or SYNOPSIS that usually includes sample DIALOGUE as well as NARRATIVE.

TRIANGLE
A collapsible three-legged device designed to hold the legs of a TRIPOD and prevent them from slipping apart. *See also SPIDER.*

TRICK PHOTOGRAPHY
See SPECIAL EFFECTS.

TRIM (n.)
Unused sections of film cut from a SCENE by the EDITOR.

TRIM (v.)
1) To CUT or shorten a SCENE during EDITING. 2) (--a light) To add a SCRIM in order to knock down the brightness.

TRIM BIN
See BIN.

TRIM TABS
See CINETABS.

TRIPACK
Color film composed of three layers of EMULSION, each one sensitive to one of the three PRIMARY COLORS. *See INTEGRAL TRIPACK.*

TRIP GEAR
An automatic timing device (called an intervalometer) that allows a camera to EXPOSE single or multiple FRAMES at a pre-arranged time, or at a steady speed. *See also TIME LAPSE PHOTOGRAPHY.*

TRIPOD
An adjustable, three-legged stand, to which a camera can be attached. The camera is attached to the tripod by the TRIPOD HEAD. There are many sizes and kinds of tripod heads including: FRICTION HEAD, GYRO HEAD, and FLUID HEAD. *See also PAN AND TILT.*

TROMBONE
An extendable clamp used to hang lights on the walls of the SET.

TRUCKING SHOT
See TRACKING SHOT, DOLLY SHOT.

T-STOP/T-NUMBER
Similar to an F-STOP, but more precise, as it is calibrated for the individual LENS, and shows the amount of light transmitted through the lens. F-stops only show the amount of light entering the lens.

TURNAROUND
A negotiated right of a WRITER or PRODUCER to submit a project to another STUDIO or NETWORK if the company at which the project

was being DEVELOPED elects not to proceed with PRODUCTION. Usually the right is subject to the condition that the developing company's investment be repaid and often that the developing company retain an interest in the film's earnings.

TURN-AROUND TIME
The minimum and specific number of free time that must be given according to UNION contract before that person may return to work without incurring a penalty. For example, an actor must be given 58 hours between completion of work Friday before beginning again on Monday. *See also FORCED CALL.*

TURRET
A revolving LENS MOUNT used in the old days before ZOOM lenses, especially on TV cameras and 16mm cameras. Lenses mounted on a turret can be swung rapidly into position by rotating the mount. *See also RACK.*

TVQ
Abbreviation for television *quotient*. It is a controversial rating system (that TV executives don't even admit using) using an unwritten set of qualifications (standards) to judge the acceptability of an actor based upon his/her likeability and recognition by TV audiences. The higher the ratings, the more acceptable to the NETWORKS. Lucille Ball, Bob Hope, Carol Burnett and Mary Tyler Moore are examples of personalities who rate high in both categories.

TWO-SHOT
A close camera shot just wide enough to keep two people within the limits of the FRAME.

TYPECAST
To select an ACTOR for a ROLE because of his or her similarity to the character, or because he/she has played a similar part before For example, casting Willie Nelson as a country singer, or Roger Moore as an international spy *(e.g., THE SAINT, James Bond).*

TYLER MOUNT
A device used to attach a camera to a helicopter or camera plane. It is equipped with a GYRO to eliminate vibration.

U

UHER
Brand name of a small, sensitive audio tape recorder used for LOCATION shooting, though not too much anymore. *See also NAGRA.*

ULTRAVIOLET
Light that cannot be seen, but which causes a bluish cast on photographic film. *See HAZE FILTER.*

UMBRELLA *(aka BOUNCE BOARD)*
A REFLECTOR that is used to bounce illumination onto a subject. This tends to produce softer lighting, with less chance of a HOT SPOT.

UNDERCRANK
A term originated in the days before sound when motion picture cameras were cranked by hand, meaning to shoot a SCENE at slower than normal speed to produce ACCELERATED MOTION.

UNDERDEVELOPED
NEGATIVE film that has been given too little time in the DEVELOPER, or has been PROCESSED in solutions at the wrong temperature, producing a THIN NEGATIVE.

UNDEREXPOSED
Film that has been subjected to too little light, or subjected to light for too short a time. The result is a THIN NEGATIVE.

UNDERGROUND FILM
A term used in the late 50's through early 70's to describe films produced independently of STUDIOS or without major financial support, whose subject matter was considered experimental, subversive, bohemian or of interest to only a small, special group.

UNDERLINE
See SCRIPT BREAKDOWN.

UNDERSHOOT
The opposite of OVERSHOOT. To shoot insufficient FOOTAGE for adequate COVERAGE of a SCENE. Although the tendency today is to overshoot (BUDGET willing), undershooting can be more disastrous. The lack of necessary footage usually doesn't show up until POST PRODUCTION when it may be impossible, or prohibitively expensive, to go back for PICK UP SHOTS to cover the missing material. A knowledgeable SCRIPT SUPERVISOR working in conjunction with the EDITOR should be able to avoid this situation.

UNDERWATER HOUSING
A special, waterproof container for a camera that allows safe shooting in and under the water.

UNDERWATER PHOTOGRAPHY
A branch of photography that, through the use of special cameras, lights, LENSES and HOUSINGS, permits shooting in and under the water.

UNION *(aka GUILD)*
A labor organization that determines work standards, wages, hours CREDITS, etc., on behalf of its members. Depending on how strong and well-organized the union/guild is, it may also offer legal advice, health and pension benefits, dental plan, have an internship program, a film society, etc.

UNION CARD
The identification slip issued to each dues paying member in good standing. The member should be able to produce his card when working on a PRODUCTION.

UNIT
The CREW working on a motion picture.

UNIT MANAGER
A production department member assigned to act as local business and production head of a particular film UNIT *(e.g., SECOND UNIT while shooting on LOCATION)*. Also another term used for UPM.

UNIT PRODUCTION MANAGER *(aka PRODUCTION MANAGER, abbr. UPM)*
The PRODUCER'S executive assigned to the PRODUCTION, responsible for coordinating and supervising all administrative, financial and technical details of the production, and overseeing the activities of the entire CREW.

UNIVERSAL LEADER
Film leader attached to the beginning and end of each REEL of RELEASE PRINTS. It corresponds to CUE MARKS in the picture just before the end of each reel to assist the PROJECTIONIST in making CHANGEOVERS. It is rapidly replacing ACADEMY LEADER.

UNSQUEEZE
A film that has been shot with an ANAMORPHIC LENS must be projected with another anamorphic lens so that it can be viewed properly. *See also WIDE SCREEN.*

UP FRONT
Before PRODUCTION begins *(e.g., a PRODUCER makes a DEAL to receive money up front from a STUDIO)*.

UPSTAGE (n.)
The BACKGROUND portion of a SET (or a stage), the part that is farthest away from the camera (or audience).

UPSTAGE (v.)
The intentional or unintentional blocking of one actor by another from the camera, or a distracting gesture or facial expression that causes the audience's attention to focus on that actor. To steal a scene. Children and animals are notorious upstagers.

UTILITY MAN
A member of the CREW (usually on videotape PRO-DUCTIONS) who assists various departments on the SET.

V

VARIABLE-AREA SOUND TRACK
An OPTICAL sound track in which the impulses are recorded as horizontal bars, varying in density from black to light grey. *See OPTICAL SOUND TRACK.*

VARIABLE FOCUS LENS
See ZOOM LENS.

VARIABLE SHUTTER
A special shutter, expressed in degrees of opening, used to control EXPOSURE of film to light. It can be used in making FADES and DISSOLVES in the camera as it has two APERTURE plates: one stationary and one moveable.

VARIABLE-SPEED MOTOR *(aka WILD MOTOR)*
A camera motor that can be run from 4 FPS to50 FPS, for use in shooting SLOW MOTION or ACCELERATED MOTION. *See also OVERCRANK, UNDERCRANK.*

VAULT
A temperature and humidity-level controlled storage area that is fireproofed in which film (generally NEGATIVES, but sometimes PRINTS as well) or tape is stored for safe-keeping.

VEHICLE
Any car, truck, motorcycle, etc., used on the PRODUCTION. *See also PICTURE CAR, TRANSPORTATION.*

VELOCILATOR
A camera support made to lift a camera, CAMERA OPERATOR and FOCUS PULLER up to six feet in the air. Some are powered, others are moved by hand. *See also DOLLY, CRANE.*

VIDEO
1) An electronic IMAGE-making system recorded on magnetic tape, usually used in television, commercials and music videos (as well as home use). 2) The visual part of a tape. *See also AUDIO.*

VIDEO ASSIST
A system often used on large BUDGET PRODUCTIONS these days where video tape is shot simultaneously with film, through the LENS of the principal camera, in order to view SCENES immediately after they are shot.

VIEWER
A device for looking at film. *See MOVIOLA, KEM, STEENBECK.*

VIEWFINDER
The part of the camera used to compose the IMAGE. Some viewfinders are separate form the picture-taking LENS, while other cameras combine the viewfinder and lens. These days most viewfinders are not separate, but are through-the-lens. *See also RACKOVER, PARALLAX.*

VISUAL EFFECTS
A term generally used to mean SPECIAL EFFECTS, but can also include special LAB work, special LIGHTING, SETS, FILTERS and PUSHED film - all of which contribute to achieving a certain look. Many times on large budget PRODUCTIONS, there is a Visual (Effects) Consultant or Director.

VOICE OVER *(Abbr. VO)*
DIALOGUE or NARRATION which comes from OFF SCREEN - the source of the voice is not seen.

WA
Abbreviation for WIDE ANGLE.

WALLAH
Background-people noise, indistinguishable voices.*See WILD SOUND*.

WAIVER
To give up something that, contractually, is called for.

WALKIE-TALKIE
Two-way communication device. Generally, these are used on the SET by the ASSISTANT DIRECTORS in order to transmit information and requests quickly.

WALK-ON
A BIT part in a film or play. *See also SILENT BIT*.

WALK-THROUGH
See RUN-THROUGH.

WARDROBE
Any item of clothing worn by an actor in a film, play or television show.

WARDROBE MISTRESS/MASTER
See COSTUMER.

WARNING BELL
One ring means shooting is about to commence and there should be QUIET ON THE SET. Two rings means all clear - shooting has stopped.   2) A signal to alert the PROJECTIONIST that a CHANGEOVER is approaching.

WASH
The water/bath that removes all DEVELOPER and fixer from film that has just been PROCESSED.

WAXING
Wax applied to the edges of new films so that they run smoothly through the PROJECTOR.

WEAVE
Unwanted sideways movement of the film in the PROJECTOR or camera.

WEB
Slang for NETWORK.

WEDGE *(aka CINEX STRIP)*
A test strip provided by the LAB that comes with the DAILIES, to indicate the range of densities possible for that negative, and to enable the CAMERAMAN to see the accuracy of the EXPOSURE.

WELFARE WORKER/TEACHER
A person who is in charge of following and maintaining the strict rules governing the working conditions of minors. *See CHILD ACTORS.*

WESTERN
The most uniquely American genre of film, featuring cowboys, Indians, horses, good guys, bad guys, etc. These films take place in the West (hence the name) and usually deal with themes like rugged individualism, the struggle between good and evil, the vanishing frontier, the American Dream, etc. John Ford and Howard Hawks were the great masters of this genre. Sergio Leone was the king of the SPAGHETTI WESTERNS.

WESTERN DOLLY
A camera platform with large rubber wheels which allows smooth, guided movement over rough, bumpy surfaces.

WET GATE
See LIQUID GATE.

WHIP SHOT
See SWISH PAN.

WHIRLY
See CRANE.

WIDE ANGLE
A SHOT that encompasses and area of 60 to 65 degrees or more, which is more than a normal LENS would see and requires the use of a WIDE ANGLE LENS.

WIDE ANGLE LENS
A convex lens which tends to emphasize the convergence of parallel lines in the distance and, therefore, the sense of depth. Objects in the FOREGROUND tend to appear disproportionately large when the lens is extremely wide angle, while objects in the background tend to appear disproportionately small. Standard lenses usually cover a range of between 45 to 50 degrees. Wide angles cover from 60 to 65 degrees and up. 35mm lenses are standard wide angle (without too much distortion) used for ANAMORPHIC systems, while 24mm lenses are used for regular spherical systems that shoot in 1.85:1. FISHEYE lenses start at 17mm and go down to 10mm, or even 8mm, with increasing distortion.

WIDE-SCREEN PROCESSES
Filming and PROJECTION systems that produce a broader than normal IMAGE. *See ASPECT RATIO, CINEMA-SCOPE, ANAMORPHIC, SCREEN, PANAVISION 70.*

WIGWAG *(aka WARNING LIGHT)*
A light, usually red, outside a SOUND STAGE indicating that SHOOTING is in progress and no one should interrupt.

WILD MOTOR
See VARIABLE SPEED MOTOR.

WILD PICTURE
Film shot without sound. *See MOS.*

WILD SOUND/WILD RECORDING
Sound recorded without picture. Usually, these sounds are the natural sounds (WALLAH, ROOM TONE, OFF-CAMERA DIALOGUE) found at a particular location which will make the SCENE more real when they are MIXED in later. *See also SOUND EFFECTS.*

WILD TRACK
See WILD SOUND.

WIND
Specifically, A-WIND or B-WIND. This refers to the way the film is wound onto the CORE: EMULSION side up or emulsion side down. In 35 mm, the winds are standardized because there are two sets of SPROCKET HOLES. A-wind (emulsion down) is used for PRINTING while B-wind is used in the camera for shooting. When going through multiple GENERATIONS between NEGATIVE and RELEASE PRINT, each generation is the opposite wind from the previous one. Sixteen millimeter film has sprocket holes on only one side of the film, and REVERSAL film is used for shooting. The concept of Winds gets very intricate with 16mm. For more information, it is best to consult a motion picture film LABORATORY.

WINDING
Moving film (or tape) from one REEL to another, or back onto its original reel or CORE. *See also REWIND.*

WIND MACHINE *(aka RITTER)*
A turbine engine or fan used to produce the effects of wind in a SCENE. *See also SPECIAL EFFECTS, STUNT COORDINATOR.*

WINDS
See WIND.

WING IT
To IMPROVISE, make something up spontaneously. *See also AD-LIB.*

WIPE
An OPTICAL EFFECT achieved in POST-PRODUCTION where one IMAGE is replaced by another as if the first were actually being wiped off the screen by the second. The manner in which the two images interface is virtually unlimited. *See also OPTICAL PRINTER.*

WORD OF MOUTH
Reaction to a film (either positive or negative) passed along by people to their friends, co-workers, etc. Many times, word of mouth can make or break a film. *See also SLEEPER.*

WORKING TITLE
The temporary name given to a film until a final name has been chosen. Sometimes, working titles are used until just before release so as to preserve secrecy and prevent piracy. For example, *ET: THE EXTRA-TERRESTRIAL* was titled *A BOY'S LIFE* until just before its release. Most of Woody Allen's films have the working title of *WOODY ALLEN MOVIE.*

WORK PRINT
An UNTIMED PRINT assembled from DAILIES with TAPE SPLICES. When the work print reaches the FINAL CUT stage, the NEGATIVE is CONFORMED to it.

WRAP
Generally, it refers to the end of a day's shooting, but can also specifically refer to the completion of a particular assignment or LOCATION, and to the end of PRINCIPAL PHOTOGRAPHY.

WRITERS GUILD OF AMERICA *(Abbr. WGA)*
The official collective bargaining union for SCREENWRITERS in the motion picture and television industry.

WRITTEN BY
A WGA designation meaning original STORY and SCREENPLAY BY.

X-Y-Z

X
1) Abbreviation for a single FRAME. 2) Number of times *(e.g., "Transfer this track 3X.")*

X-COPY
First duplicate TRANSFERRED SOUND MASTER.

X-DISSOLVE
Abbreviation for CROSS-DISSOLVE.

XFR/XFER
Abbreviation for TRANSFER.

XLS
Abbreviation for EXTRA LONG SHOT.

X-RATED
A motion picture only for people over the age of 21. Although some X-ratings have been given for excessive violence, most are given for depicting explicit sex.

Y-CABLE/Y-JOINT
A two-pronged electrical connecting unit with plugs/ connectors at all three ends.

YELLOW
One of the PRIMARY COLORS .

ZEPPELIN *(aka ZEPPELIN WINDSCREEN)*
A tube attached to a SHOTGUN microphone with perforations to limit wind noise.

ZIP PAN
See SWISH PAN.

ZOETROPE
An early, circular device, before the days of motion pictures, for viewing a series of pictures that turned and gave the illusion of motion.

ZOOM
A method of changing the relative size of the subject in an IMAGE by changing the FOCAL LENGTH of a subject (only on a ZOOM LENS). This is accompanied by a change in the DEPTH OF FIELD. When the camera ZOOMS IN , the subject appears to become larger and the depth of field is lessened. When the camera ZOOMS OUT, the subject becomes smaller and the depth of field increases. When the camera moves in and out on a DOLLY, the depth of field remains the same.

ZOOM LENS
A lens with variable FOCAL LENGTHS, generally used on motion picture and video cameras combining normal, WIDE ANGLE and TELEPHOTO lenses in a single unit. A zoom lens eliminates the need to change lenses ever time a new focal length is desired. The zoom lens also has the ability to zoom in and out, changing the size of the IMAGE relative to the position of the camera, without having to refocus. The zoom lens does, however have its disadvantages. Generally, the quaity is less good than PRIME LENSES, and they have slower speeds. *See also ZOOM.*
